COMPANION
JOURNAL

DEEPER THINKING IN THE CLASSROOM:
A PRACTICAL GUIDE TO THE CREATE METHOD

www.curiosity2create.org

Design by Sally Barlow

www.curiosity2create.org

ISBN: 979-8-9897654-6-1

First printing edition 2024

EDLINKS® Press LLC
PO Box 205
Essex Junction, VT 05453
USA
www.edlinks.com/edlinks-press

For information about purchases, special requests, and educational needs, contact EDLINKS® Press at edlinkspress@edlinks.com or visit Curiosity 2 Create at www.curiosity2create.org.

DISCOVER THE JOY OF TEACHING AND EMBRACING YOUR CREATIVITY WITH THE CREATE METHOD!

As educators, we know that teaching is more than just a job—it's a calling. And we should never forget that teachers are humans with lives outside the classroom.

This journal is designed to allow you to refresh your soul, find joy in simple pleasures, and nurture your creative spirit. It will remind you to laugh with friends, celebrate with family, and infuse creativity into every aspect of your life.

Join us on this journey as we explore how to bring creativity not only into your classroom but also into your personal lives. Let this journal inspire you to embrace your ability to be fiercely creative.

HOW TO USE THIS COMPANION

Ready for weeks of creativity and growth?

Here's what to expect:

• Weekly Check-ins: Start your week with a quick self-assessment to set the tone. Create a weekly affirmation here also. For example, "I am growing."

• Journals: Use inspiring quotes to encourage reflection and challenge your thinking.

• Activities: Have fun with creative activities throughout the week to help you relax and recharge or connect with friends and family.

 See a page with lightbulb? Take some time to learn something new.

 See a page with a pencil? Take some time to do something new.

GET READY TO MAKE EACH WEEK A LITTLE BRIGHTER AND FIERCELY CREATIVE!

THIS YEAR _____

I AM TEACHING:

MY HOME LIFE IS:

I LOVE TO WATCH:

MY FAVORITE SONG IS:

MY PERSONAL GOALS ARE:

- _____
- _____
- _____
- _____
- _____

MY PROFESSIONAL GOALS ARE:

- _____
- _____
- _____
- _____
- _____

MY BIGGEST STRENGTH IN THE CLASSROOM IS:

MY BIGGEST WEAKNESS IN THE CLASSROOM IS:

THE

METHOD

CONTENT CURATOR

Content curation is the practice of gathering and organizing information meaningfully with the goal of igniting curiosity in students. Using The CREATE Method will assist educators in determining the most valuable and meaningful content to use in a unit.

RISK FACILITATOR

Many students and teachers hesitate to express new or contrasting ideas out of fear of failure and judgment. With CREATE, we aim to change that mindset. This segment encourages you to embrace ambiguity and be open-minded. We're here to show you the significance of deferring judgment.

EXPERIENCE NAVIGATOR

Brace yourselves for captivating, inquiry-based, problem-solving units! With The CREATE Method, you can personalize your classroom experience by engaging and challenging your students uniquely.

ATTITUDE SHIFTER

Adopting a curious and creative mindset requires shifting how we perceive the learning process, ourselves, and others. The CREATE Method explores the impact a creative classroom environment has on building engagement.

TEAM TRANSFORMER

Getting accustomed to a creative environment allows team members to become more robust, efficient, and confident communicators and collaborators. The CREATE Method provides invaluable tools and strategies to transform communication skills and enhance team effectiveness.

EVALUATION DESIGNER

Assessing skills like creativity and curiosity can be challenging. This section of The CREATE Method will teach you how to provide opportunities for students to take ownership of their learning and design meaningful assessments.

WHAT IS CREATIVITY?

SECTION 1

Creativity is seeing what others see and thinking what no one else ever thought.
~ Albert Einstein

THE JOURNEY OF LIVING CREATIVELY

Teaching is shaping tomorrow's visionaries. The essence of being an effective teacher lies in a skill you rarely get graded for on the syllabus. It's creativity. The downright fierce and deliberate creativity that lights up a classroom and makes students' eyes sparkle with endless possibilities.

WHAT IS CREATIVITY ANYWAY?

In the universe of learning, creativity is akin to the rich soil that allows a garden to grow and thrive. This is not just a shift from Blackboard to PowerPoint when discussing creative teaching. This is the dynamic fusion of imagination, innovation, and insight that blazes a trail for a paradigm shift in education.

Why should creativity be at the forefront of a teacher's personal and professional mission? Because creativity is not just about inventing new concepts; it's about understanding the familiar in unfamiliar ways. When we engage with our creative selves, we problem-solve, empathize, and think more critically.

THE MENTAL HEALTH CONNECTION

When harnessed as a teaching tool, creativity is not just important—it is essential. Creativity in the classroom has a direct relationship with mental health. Students are not cookie-cutter molds, and expecting them to learn within rigid confines often leads to frustration and disengagement. Incorporating creative elements into your teaching reignites the excitement for learning and fuels the students' mental well-being.

Just as importantly, a classroom that fosters creativity is a workplace that encourages experimentation and adaptability. It's an environment that honors the unique teaching styles of every educator and prevents burnout by keeping lesson plans from becoming stagnant. It's a classroom that brings joy.

LIVING WITH YOUR CREATIVITY

It's one thing to acknowledge the importance of creativity; it's another to weave it into the very fabric of your being. It is not just for either your personal or professional work, it is needed in all aspects of life. Imagine a classroom where every subject is taught in the spirit of creative exploration; this is the vision of a life with deliberate creativity.

How to bring creativity to life

STAY CURIOUS

- Be insatiably curious. Curiosity fuels the imagination and is the spark of every creative fire.

- Learn something new daily, whether it's a new teaching methodology or a random fact that intrigues you.

- Encourage the same curiosity in your students, and you'll find that their natural enthusiasm for learning is the crucible for creative growth.

- It seems obvious, but allow the space for questions. We tend to rush through them to stay on task and on time, but by giving questions space in our room, and student permission to be askers of them, we are teaching them a lifelong skill that is necessary or critical thinking as an adult.

THINK ABOUT:

1. How have I nurtured my curiosity today, and how can I continue to cultivate it?

2. How can I empower my students to embrace their role as question-askers and engage in critical thinking?

3. What resources or opportunities can I seek out to further develop my curiosity and expand my knowledge base?

4. How can I model a curious mindset for my students and peers, demonstrating the value of lifelong learning and intellectual curiosity?

THINK DIFFERENTLY AND BE OPEN-MINDED

- Look at things from a different perspective. Different angles and different perspectives give entirely different information.

- Be bold and challenge traditional thinking and the established curriculum. By thinking differently, you will find other ways to impart knowledge. Much has changed since the way "we have always done it" was started.

- Invite your students to do the same; show them that creativity is not a luxury but a necessary tool in their intellectual toolkit.

THINK ABOUT:

1. Have I explored alternative perspectives or unconventional approaches to a particular concept or subject matter?

2. What steps can I take to create a learning environment that values and celebrates diverse perspectives and unconventional thinking?

3. Reflecting on past experiences, how has thinking differently led to positive outcomes?

4. How can I challenge the status quo and question established norms or beliefs? How can I shake things up and inject fresh perspectives?

TAKE RISKS

- Start your day with the spirit of an experimenter. Try new things with gusto and an open mind.

- Accept that some approaches may yield different results than expected, but each brings you closer to the method that will resonate with you.
  This willingness to experiment will inspire you and your students to take risks and try new things.

- Remind your students (and maybe yourself) that failure provides valuable information, it's not wrong, it is a way of learning, and it should be valued.

THINK ABOUT:

1. Have I embraced the mindset of an experimenter today, approaching my day with openness and enthusiasm for trying new things?

2. Have I accepted that some of my experiments may yield unexpected results, and how have I leveraged these outcomes as opportunities for growth and learning?

3. Reflecting on past experiments, what have been some of the most valuable lessons I've learned from approaches that didn't go as planned?

4. What strategies can I employ to maintain a sense of curiosity and openness to experimentation throughout the school day, even when faced with challenges or setbacks?

COLLABORATE CREATIVELY

- Seek out partnerships with other teachers, local artists, or community leaders.

- Lead projects that break the bounds of conventional teaching, leaving a lasting impression on your students.

- Encourage teamwork in your classes. That is how most adults work, and school is a great place to learn that skill.

THINK ABOUT:

1. How actively have I sought partnerships with others to enrich the learning experiences of my students?

2. Have I fostered a culture of teamwork, recognizing its importance as a fundamental skill for success in the world?

3. Reflecting on recent collaborative efforts, what successes have emerged, and what lessons have I learned from any challenges faced?

4. How have partnerships with other educators or community members influenced my own professional growth and teaching practices?

CELEBRATE CREATIVITY

- Make a habit of recognizing and celebrating moments of creativity.

- Praise students for unique insights, and don't fear rewarding risk-taking, especially when the result did not go as planned.

- Value creativity to create an environment in which it can flourish.

- Celebrate all attempts, regardless of outcomes. Trying is more valuable than inactivity, so that is what should be reinforced.

THINK ABOUT:

1. How have I celebrated and acknowledged any efforts and attempts, even when these may not have succeeded as expected?

2. How can I model a mindset that embraces failure as a natural part of the learning process?

3. What opportunities can I create to showcase and celebrate creative achievements, both within the classroom and beyond?

4. How can I continue to evolve as a teacher to better support and nurture the creativity of all my students, regardless of their backgrounds or abilities?

Reflect and Adapt

- Look back at what worked and what didn't, and be willing to make changes.

- Use questions as a feedback tool for both you and your students. Using "what might be all the ways this could be done differently" is open ended and allows for the person to see mistakes as belonging to the situation, not their personality.

- Reflect on your personal and professional practices, and you set the stage for continuous creative evolution in your everyday life.

THINK ABOUT:

1. Reflecting on recent experiences, how have I responded to mistakes or challenges, viewing them as opportunities for growth rather than personal failures?

2. What strategies can I implement to encourage a culture of open dialogue and constructive feedback in my life?

3. Have I actively sought out feedback from colleagues or mentors to gain insight into areas for improvement in my teaching practice?

4. What steps can I take to reflect on both my personal and professional practices regularly, fostering continuous creative evolution in my teaching approach?

WEEKLY CHECK IN

Choose at least three days this week you will spend doing something creative.

◯ ◯ ◯ ◯ ◯ ◯ ◯
s m t w t f s

This week I'm going to focus on creativity by:

1. _____

2. _____

3. _____

Three things I am grateful for:

1. _____

2. _____

3. _____

WEEKLY AFFIRMATION:

CHALLENGE OF THE WEEK

List all the different areas you see creativity throughout the week.

_____

_____

_____

_____

_____

Personal goals for this week:

_____

_____

_____

Professional goals for this week:

_____

_____

_____

ADD IN EVERYTHING YOU KNOW ABOUT CREATIVITY.
COME BACK AND ADD MORE BUBBLES AS YOU LEARN MORE.

WRITE IN ALL THE WAYS CREATIVITY CAN BE USED IN YOUR CLASSROOM. ADD MORE BUBBLES WHEN YOU THINK OF MORE PLACES AND TIMES.

IDEA BUILDING

STEP 1 What might be all the pictures you can draw using the circles below?

STEP 2 Now look around the room for ideas, not to mimic, but to build off of or add to your artwork.

STEP 3 Allow your mind to wander, consider all the places where there are circles and add them to your artwork.

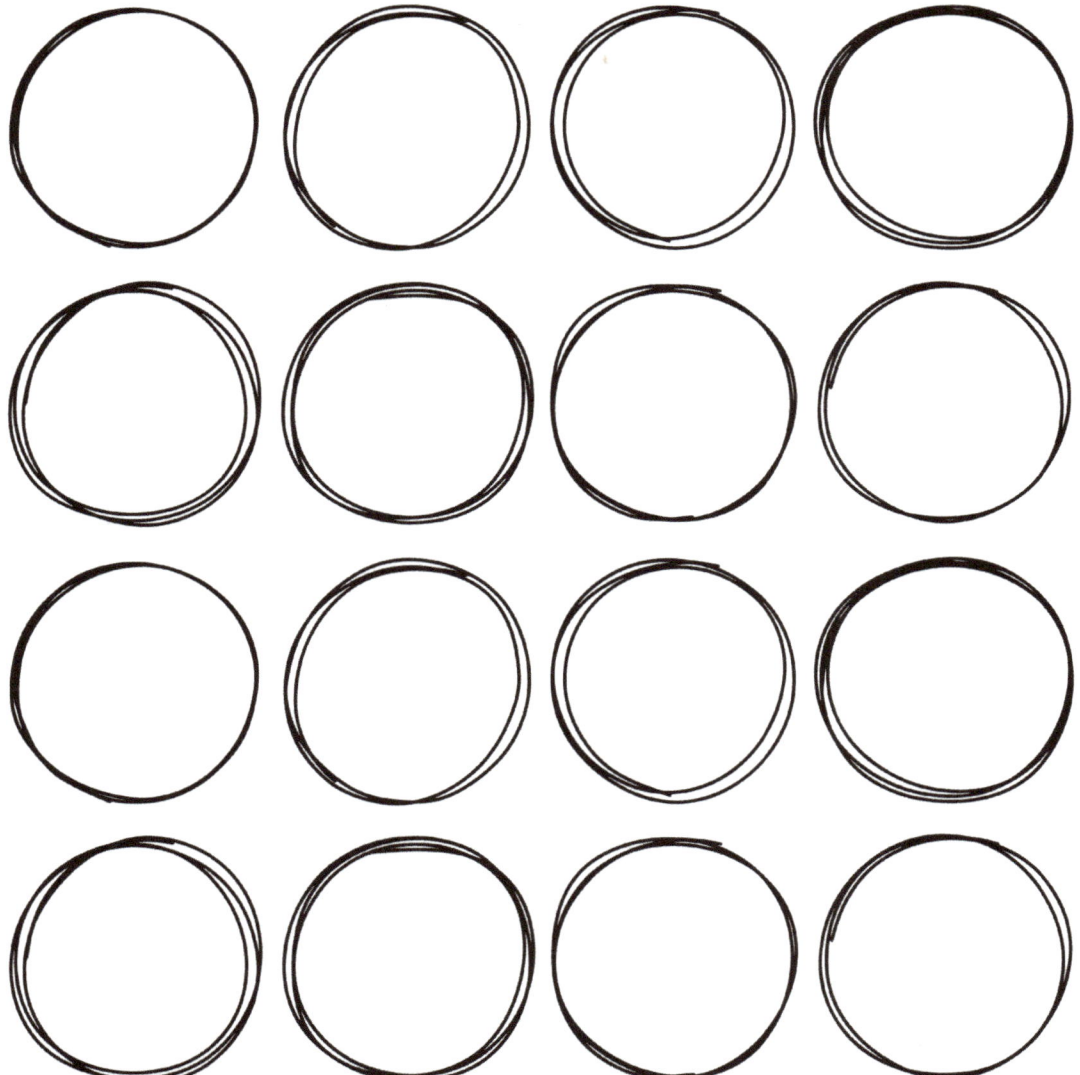

REFLECT

What were some challenges to the process? What did you like about it? Did any of your artwork surprise you? Did you stay inside the circle or did you go outside of it? What unsaid rules did you impose on your drawings? How do you feel about your creativity afterward? Did you have fun or feel relaxed?

Practicing the circle activity helps prime your brain for generating numerous and diverse ideas. Think of it as warming up your brain, akin to how a runner prepares before a sprint. This is imporant to think about when planning activities in our classroom. Are we warming up for the kind of thinking we want our students to be doing?

These are some examples of brain warm ups. See how well you do.

What might be all the ways to get a hippo out of your bathtub?

_____

_____

_____

_____

_____

_____

_____

_____

_____

_____

_____

_____

What might be all the uses for a million lightbulbs?

_____

_____

_____

_____

_____

_____

_____

_____

_____

_____

_____

_____

If you could create the PERFECT desk, and rules of logic and physics did not apply, what might be all the things you would add or change?

_____

_____

_____

_____

_____

_____

_____

_____

_____

_____

_____

_____

As we walk through this creative journey together, you will reflect on the past, celebrate the present, and imagine the future. Creativity means being open-minded to all perspectives and finding joy during the process. What are you most looking forward to?

_____

_____

_____

_____

_____

_____

_____

_____

_____

_____

_____

_____

_____

_____

_____

"Creativity is inventing, experimenting, growing, taking risks,
breaking rules, making mistakes, and having fun."

~ Mary Lou Cook

YES, YOU ARE CREATIVE

Many mistakenly believe that they lack creativity, but the truth is, everyone possesses it. Asking probing questions, planning vacations or home renovations, finding alternative routes in traffic – all showcase creativity. Simply navigating through daily life demands creative thinking. Embrace your inner creativity; it's more prevalent than you realize.

Creativity is not limited to those who are considered "artists." Creativity can be found in all aspects of life. As a teacher, you must constantly develop new and innovative ways to engage your students. Scientists use creative thinking to solve complex problems, and single parents have to think creatively to manage their time and resources effectively.

Consider all the things that you have done that you can now see are creative. Add as many lines as you need to when you think about all the roles that you have been creative in and all the situations that have required your creativity. Come back and add to this list as often as you like.

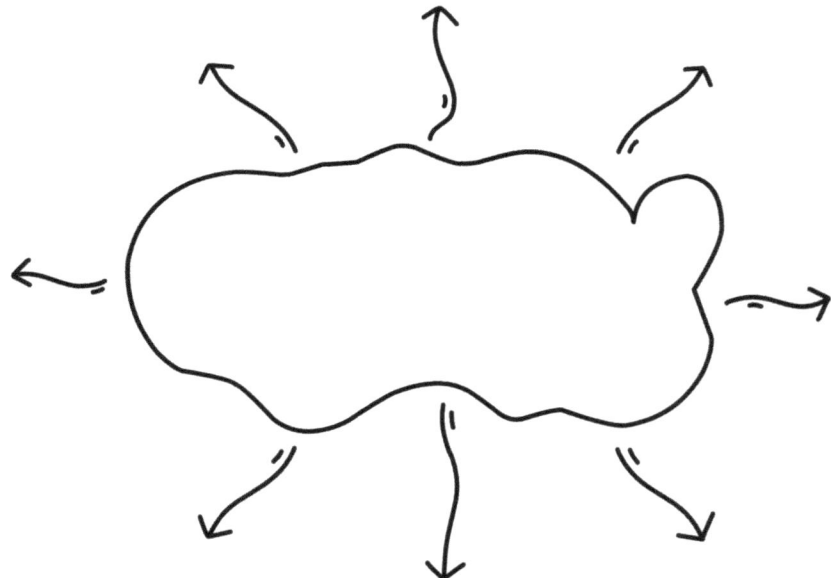

ON A SCALE, HOW ARE YOU CREATIVE?

We usually think in terms of level when it comes to creativity, but since we now know that everyone is creative, think about the style of creativity that you have.

$\longleftrightarrow$

Adaptive, I modify things into a new thing

Innovative, I break boundaries and wildly expand on what people accept as "normal"

WHEN WAS A TIME YOU BELIEVED YOU WERE CREATIVE?

WHAT DID IT LOOK LIKE?

HOW DID IT FEEL?

"A creative life is an amplified life. It's a bigger life, a happier life, an expanded life, and a hell of a lot more interesting life."

~ Elizabeth Gilbert

WRITE IN ALL THE WAYS CREATIVITY CAN BE USED IN YOUR PERSONAL LIFE. ADD MORE BUBBLES WHEN YOU THINK OF MOREPLACES AND TIMES.

"My contention is that creativity now is as important in education as literacy, and we should treat it with the same status."

~ Sir Ken Robinson

Do you agree that creativity is as important as literacy? What might we do, as educators, to promote the necessity of creativity in education? What might you do to promote creativity in your classroom?

_____

_____

_____

_____

_____

_____

_____

_____

_____

_____

_____

_____

_____

_____

_____

_____

WHAT IS CREATIVE PROBLEM SOLVING?

Refined and validated over decades, Creative Problem Solving (CPS) emerged from the minds of Alex Osborn and Sidney Parnes in the 1950s. This structured approach guides individuals through breaking down challenges into manageable stages and equipping them with tools and techniques at each step to foster novel solutions.

At its essence, CPS hinges on the dichotomy of divergent thinking (generating myriad ideas) and convergent thinking (selecting and refining ideas based on defined criteria). Central to its methodology is the principle of "yes, and…" thinking, which involves building upon ideas collaboratively, and framing challenges as questions to stimulate exploration.

Ruth Noller illustrated this concept mathematically, expressing creativity as a function of attitude, knowledge, imagination, and evaluation($C=fa(K,I,E)$). This equation underscores the interplay of these factors in the creative process.

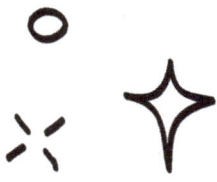

Creativity is a function of attitude, knowledge, imagination, and evaluation.

Whether in the classroom or in personal endeavors, leveraging CPS principles nurtures creativity. By instilling these guidelines, particularly in educational settings, we cultivate habits that endure throughout a lifetime. Like any skill, creativity can be cultivated, honed, and expanded upon over time.

In our personal lives, practicing creative thinking results in a multitude of benefits. It empowers us to tackle both major and minor issues with ingenuity, fosters self-awareness, and dismantles self-imposed barriers, unlocking our full potential.

Creative problem solving is based on using both divergent thinking and convergent thinking, AND (most importantly) doing them separately.

These are the guidelines for each, to help you be more successful when you are engaged in them.

Divergent Thinking

DEFER JUDGEMENT

We do not want to stifle ideas or thoughts. Editing and refining happen later, based on criteria.

STRIVE FOR QUANTITY

Push for more ideas because our first idea is rarely our best, and quality lies inside of quantity.

SEEK WILD AND UNUSUAL IDEAS

It is easier to tame something crazy into something elegant than it is to resuscitate a tired idea.

BUILD ON OTHERS' IDEAS

Different minds contribute from different experiences, and this generates new and original ideas.

DIVERGENT THINKING

1 DEFER JUDGEMENT

2 STRIVE FOR QUANTITY

3 SEEK WILD & UNUSUAL IDEAS

4 BUILD ON OTHER'S IDEAS

Adapted from Miller, B., Vehar, J., Firestein, R., Thurber, S., & Nielsen, D. (2001) Creativity unbound. Williamsville, NY: Innovative System Group

CONVERGENT Thinking

Be Affirmative

Phrase things in the positive rather than the negative. For example "I want to start..." instead of "I must stop..."

Be Deliberate

Give time to consider each idea, and give them each a chance.

Check Your Objectives

Are you heading in the right direction or did you get sidetracked?

Improve Ideas

Continuously refine and develop your ideas.

Consider Novelty

It is easy to slide back into complacency. Be sure to keep the originality and the unexpectedness in your ideas.

CONVERGENT THINKING

 **1 Be Affirmative**

 **2 Be Deliberate**

 **3 Check Your Objectives**

 **4 Improve Ideas**

 **5 Consider Novelty**

Adapted from Miller, B., Vehar, J., Firestein, R., Thurber, S., & Nielsen, D. (2001) Creativity unbound. Williamsville, NY: Innovative System Group

CREATIVITY IS A SKILL, MEANING WE CAN LEARN MORE ABOUT IT AND IMPROVE OUR EASE OF USE.

Many people feel that things aren't creative unless they are groundbreaking, but adaptive creativity is just as valuable. The first plane that flew is NOT the one that we want to fly across the country in. We appreciate the refinements over time and from experiences, and we should recognize the creativity in those.

CONSIDER HOW OFTEN YOU FEEL THAT YOU ARE BEING CREATIVE:

NOW

As you begin this journey . . .

LATER

After you have spent a week or two working in this book

WEEKLY CHECK IN

Choose at least three days this week you will spend doing something creative.

○ ○ ○ ○ ○ ○ ○
s m t w t f s

This week I'm going to focus on creativity by:

1. _____

2. _____

3. _____

Three things I am grateful for:

1. _____

2. _____

3. _____

WEEKLY AFFIRMATION:

CHALLENGE OF THE WEEK

List all the different areas you see creativity throughout the week.

_____

_____

_____

_____

_____

Personal goals for this week:

_____

_____

_____

Professional goals for this week:

_____

_____

_____

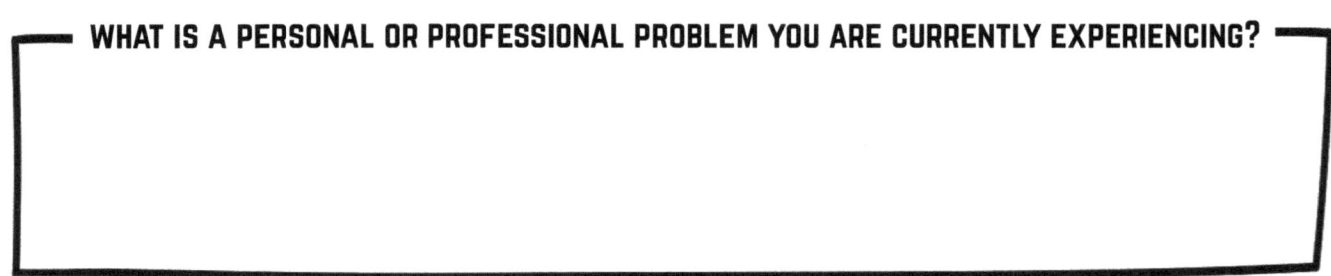

WHAT IS A PERSONAL OR PROFESSIONAL PROBLEM YOU ARE CURRENTLY EXPERIENCING?

Now rewrite that as different statements. Start with "I wish..." or "It would be great if..."
Think of all the different ways you can see this challenge.

For example:
Problem: We never have enough time to get into literacy groups.
Rewrite: I wish we had more time to get into literacy groups.
It would be great if literacy groups happened consistently each day.

I WISH...

IT WOULD BE GREAT IF...

GATHER SOME INFORMATION

Write down everything you know about this problem.

When does it occur?

_____

_____

Who does it affect?

_____

_____

How long has this been an issue?

_____

_____

What has been tried as a solution in the past?

_____

_____

What has changed since then?

_____

_____

When did it become a problem?

_____

_____

You want to understand the root of the challenge. Often we solve the symptom, not the real problem. By digging to the bottom of a problem you can create the best solution.

ALLOWING ALL OF THE INFORMATION FROM THE PREVIOUS TWO PAGES TO INFLUENCE YOUR THOUGHTS, REWRITE YOUR CHALLENGE AS A QUESTION IN SEVERAL DIFFERENT WAYS.

Pro tip - start with "How to..." or "How might..." and do not include solution ideas yet!

LOOK AT WHAT YOU HAVE WRITTEN.

CIRCLE YOUR FAVORITE.

CIRCLE THE ONE THAT SCARES YOU.

CIRCLE THE CRAZIEST ONE.

PICK ONE OF THESE QUESTIONS, OR COMBINE SOME, AND REWRITE IT HERE:

WRITE DOWN AS MANY WAYS THAT YOU CAN THINK OF TO SOLVE THIS PROBLEM.

_____

_____

_____

_____

_____

_____

_____

IMAGINE THAT YOU HAD A MAGIC WAND . . .
WRITE DOWN EVEN MORE WAYS YOU WOULD SOLVE IT WITH THAT.

_____

_____

_____

_____

_____

_____

_____

THINK OF YOUR HERO. HOW WOULD THEY SOLVE THIS?
WRITE DOWN EVEN MORE IDEAS THEY MIGHT HAVE.

_____

_____

_____

_____

_____

_____

_____

_____

LOOK AT WHAT YOU HAVE WRITTEN.

CIRCLE THREE THAT GIVE YOU TINGLES.

CIRCLE THREE THAT ARE UNEXPECTED.

CIRCLE THREE THAT YOU LOVE.

Choose from these ideas, a solution or a combination of solutions, that you want to work with and write it here. Fiddle around with it until it sounds like the best solution.
(You can always change your mind and go back.)

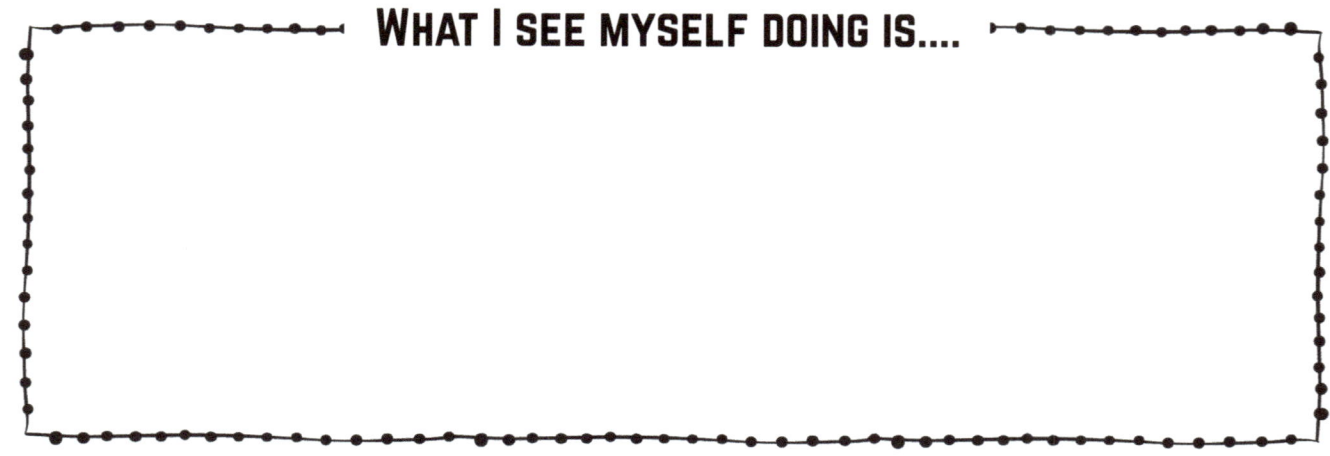

WHAT I SEE MYSELF DOING IS....

WHAT DO I LIKE ABOUT THIS SOLUTION? Write three things that excite you about it.

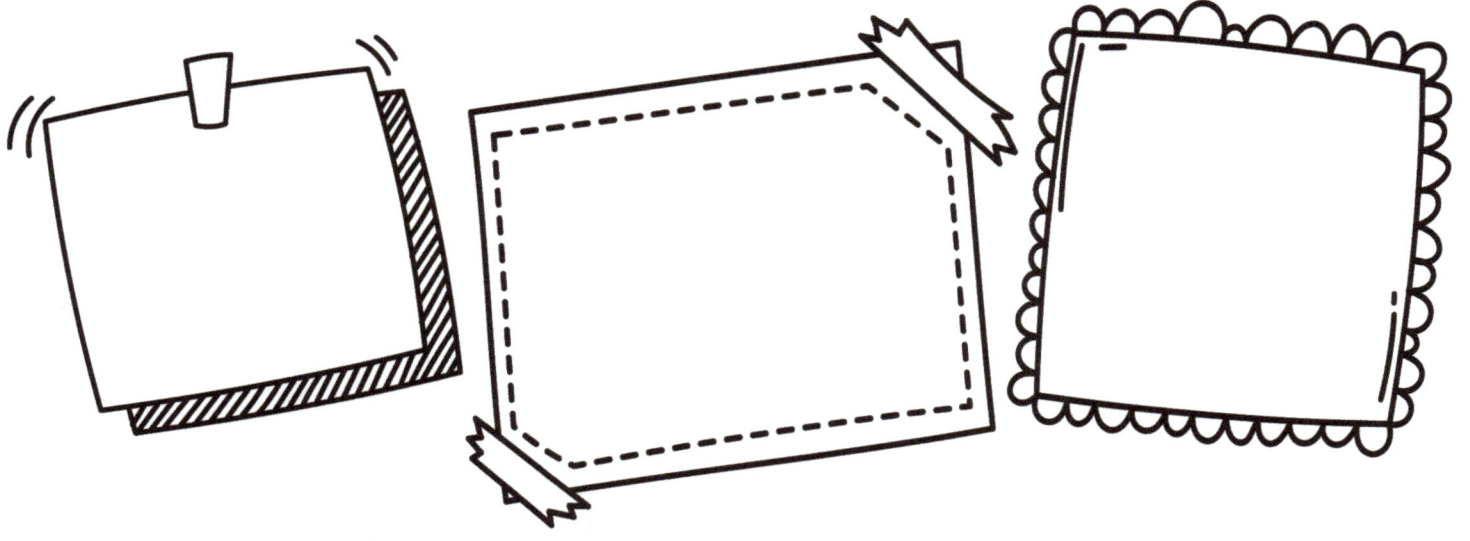

WHAT ARE SOME CONCERNS?
WHO MIGHT YOU NEED TO GET ON YOUR SIDE?
WHAT ARE SOME STUMBLING BLOCKS YOU MIGHT ENCOUNTER?

Write them as questions. Start them with "How to..." or "What might be all the ways..."

TAKE THOSE QUESTIONS AND COME UP WITH SOLUTIONS OR ANSWERS FOR THEM.

_____

_____

_____

_____

_____

_____

_____

_____

Now rewrite your solution from the previous page, adding in these refinements.

NOW WHAT I SEE MYSELF DOING IS....

WRITE EIGHT THINGS YOU WILL HAVE TO DO TO MAKE THIS HAPPEN.

_____

_____

_____

_____

_____

_____

_____

_____

Now, rewrite them in order of how they need to happen, starting with the one that you will do in the next 24 hours. Add the name of the person who you can tell you did the step.

1 _____

2 _____

3 _____

4 _____

5 _____

6 _____

7 _____

8 _____

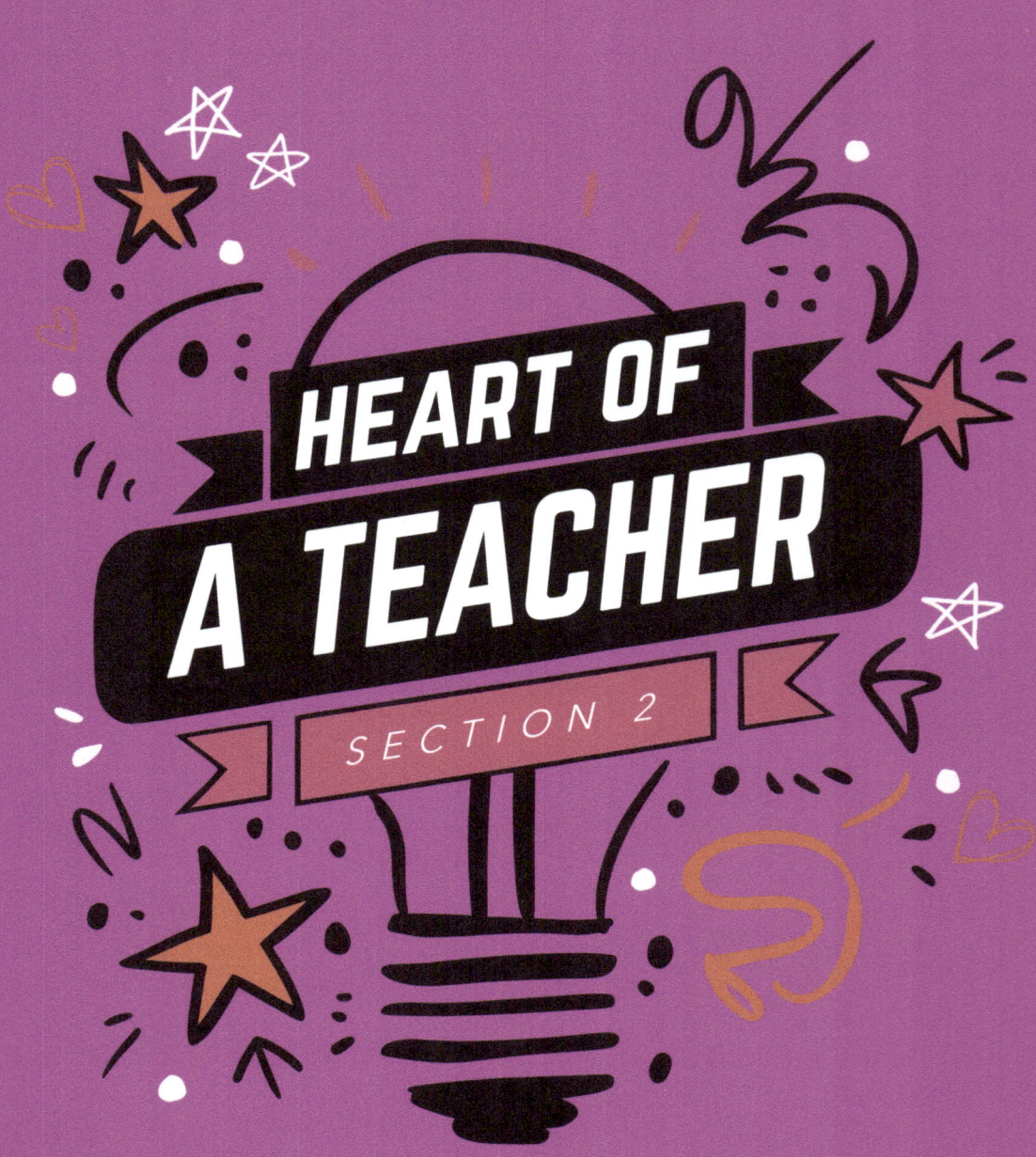

HEART OF
A TEACHER

SECTION 2

HEART OF A TEACHER

How do teachers balance the emotional demands of their profession with the need for self-care?

How does the passion for teaching shape the character of an educator?

In what ways does teaching become a form of nurturing?

Why Teachers Need Time to Refresh:

We see you and all that you do for your students and colleagues; your dedication has no limit. Yet, amidst the endless tasks of teaching–late night grading, early morning meetings, staying energetic and joyful during lessons, wiping tears, strategizing with parents and coworkers, talking with angry, apathetic, or hurt teens, and professional development–it's no surprise that you often arrive home exhausted.

This exhaustion takes a physical, emotional, and mental toll on your creativity and passion. To truly thrive as a teacher, you need time for rejuvenation. Neglecting self-care leads to decreased effectiveness, not because of incapability but because everyone needs to be refilled eventually.

Taking time for self-care is essential for personal fulfillment and professional success. Other amazing facets of your character deserve time and attention as well. Acknowledging when you feel depleted is crucial because ignoring your own needs hampers your ability to meet the needs of others effectively.

THIS SECTION AIMS TO GUIDE YOU IN RECONNECTING WITH WHO YOU ARE AND WHAT YOU LOVE, REDISCOVERING YOUR PASSIONS, AND ESTABLISHING BOUNDARIES TO SUSTAIN YOU IN YOUR CALLING AS A TEACHER.

WEEKLY CHECK IN

Choose at least three days this week you will spend doing something creative.

◯ ◯ ◯ ◯ ◯ ◯ ◯
s   m   t   w   t   f   s

This week I'm going to focus on on refreshing myself by:

1. _____

2. _____

3. _____

Three things I am grateful for:

1. _____

2. _____

3. _____

WEEKLY AFFIRMATION:

CHALLENGE OF THE WEEK

Challenge of the Week: How might I make time to rediscover who I am outside the classroom and why that makes me a good teacher?

_____

_____

_____

_____

Personal goals for this week:

_____

_____

_____

Professional goals for this week:

_____

_____

_____

WHAT SETS YOU APART FROM OTHERS? WHAT SKILLS, TALENTS, PASSIONS, OR IDEAS DO YOU HAVE?

HOW HAVE THOSE SKILLS, TALENTS, PASSIONS, OR IDEAS BRIGHTENED OR ENCOURAGED SOMEONE ELSE'S HEART?

HAVE YOU EVER BURIED ANY OF THOSE SKILLS, TALENTS, PASSIONS, OR IDEAS TO CONFORM OR FIT INTO THE EXPECTATIONS OF OTHERS? HOW COULD YOU USE YOUR STRENGTHS TO MAKE A DIFFERENCE?

WHY DID YOU BECOME A TEACHER?

Recall why you became a teacher. What motivated your decision? Was there a significant influence? Why do you continue in this profession?
Jot down all the reasons here.

Create a mission statement for your work as a teacher, similar to company mission statements. This activity can profoundly shape how you approach your day, classroom, and career. For some guidance, mission statements usually include a purpose, a group or an audience that is served, and characteristics that set you apart.

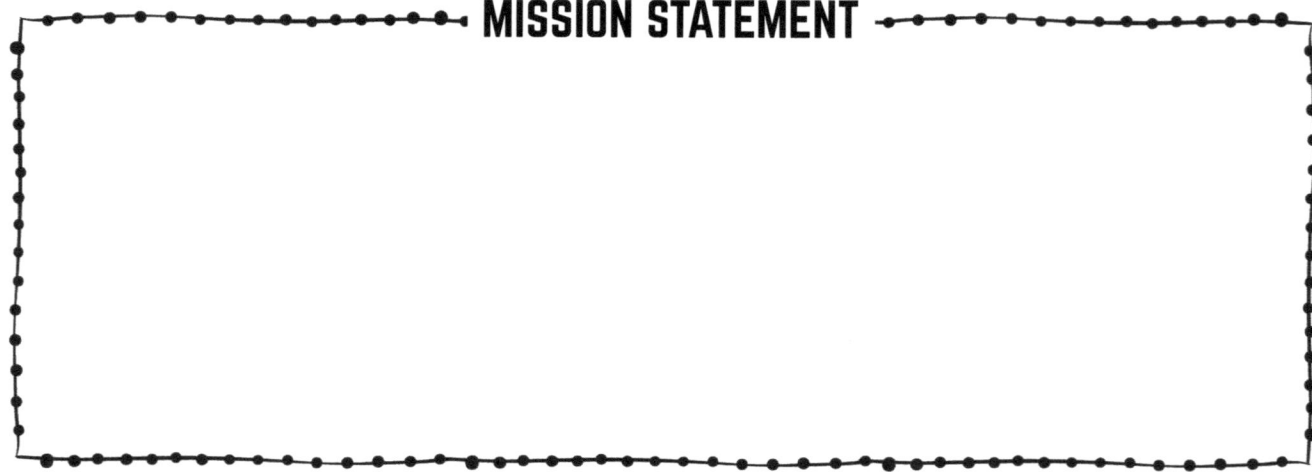

MISSION STATEMENT

Find a place to hang this in your classroom, your mirror, or your car as a daily reminder why you are here!

"Watch a teacher with a classroom full of students,
and you'll see what real love looks like."

~ Teresa Kwant

Reflect on your own experiences as an educator. Describe moments when you have witnessed or embodied this 'real love' in your teaching practice. How do you cultivate a sense of care, dedication, and mentorship in your interactions with students?

_____

_____

_____

_____

_____

_____

_____

_____

_____

_____

_____

_____

_____

_____

_____

_____

_____

_____

_____

_____

> *"A teacher affects eternity; he can never tell where his influence stops."*
>
> ~ Henry Brooks Adams

Consider the ripple effects of your teaching beyond the classroom. Fill in who has been or has the potential to be impacted by your influence.

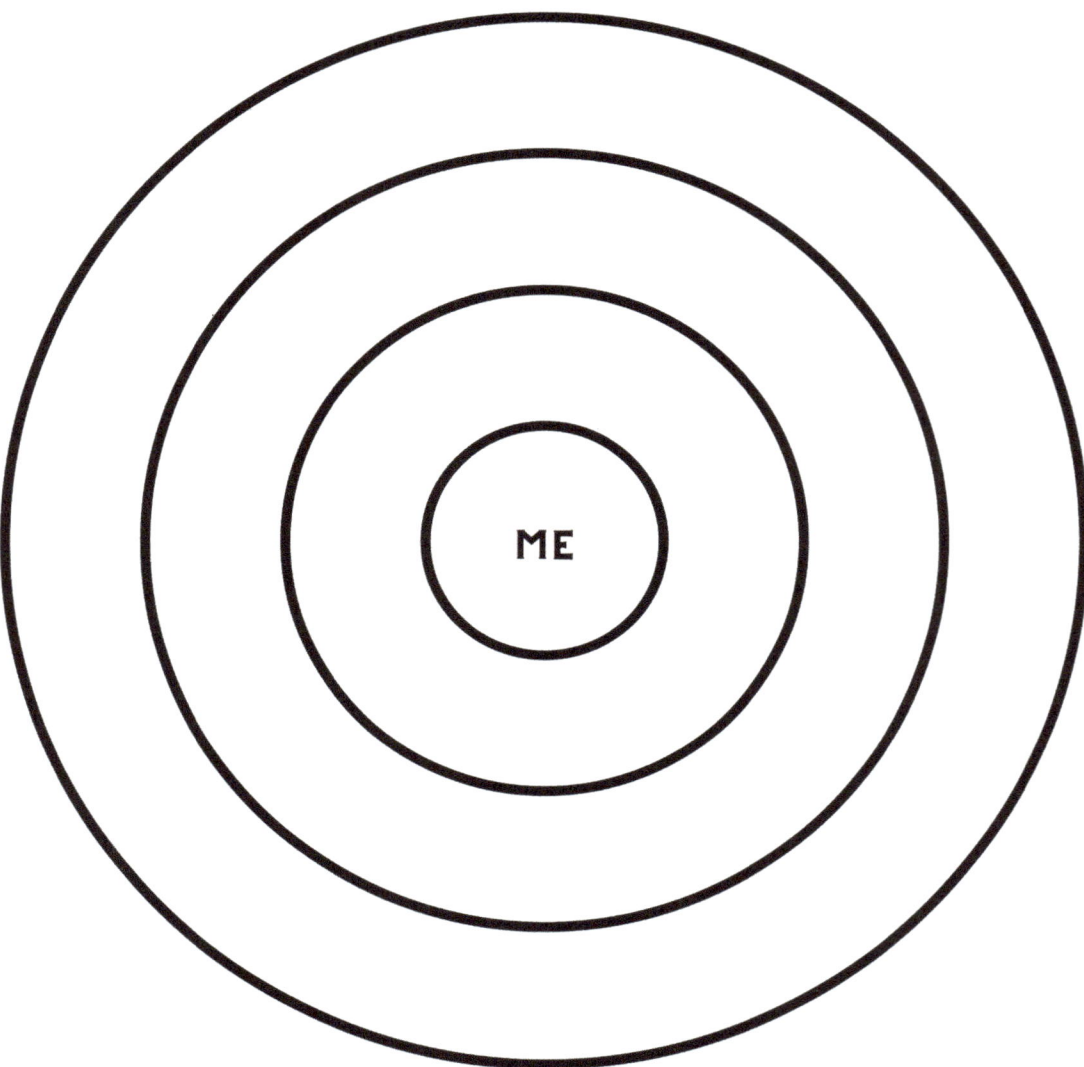

ME

Describe moments when you have felt the weight of your influence on students' lives, both past and present, or how you navigate the responsibility of shaping minds and character with a keen awareness of the long-lasting impact.

*"A good teacher can inspire hope, ignite the imagination,
and instill a love of learning."*

~ Brad Henry

Consider instances in your teaching career where you witnessed or experienced the power of inspiration, imagination, and love for learning in action. How do you cultivate these qualities within yourself as a teacher and nurture them in your students?

> *"The need for imagination, as a sense of truth, and as a feeling of responsibility –these are the three forces which are the very nerve of education."*
>
> ~ Rudolf Steiner

Explain how each of these are seen in your personal life.

NEED FOR IMAGINATION

A SENSE OF TRUTH

A FEELING OF RESPONSIBILITY

HOW DO YOU...

...As a teacher cultivate imaginations, encourage the pursuit of truth, and instill a sense of accountability with your students and colleagues?

WEEKLY CHECK IN

Choose at least three days this week you will spend doing something creative.

◯ ◯ ◯ ◯ ◯ ◯ ◯
s   m   t   w   t   f   s

This week I'm going to focus on refreshing myself by:

1. _____

2. _____

3. _____

Three things I am grateful for:

1. _____

2. _____

3. _____

WEEKLY AFFIRMATION:

CHALLENGE OF THE WEEK

How might I schedule my week to make time for something I really love doing?

_____
_____
_____
_____
_____

Personal goals for this week:

_____
_____
_____
_____

Professional goals for this week:

_____
_____
_____
_____

WHERE DOES THE TIME GO?

Track your time and create a pie chart of how your time is spent and the activities you participate in. Note which tasks boost your energy and which ones drain it.

Put a star next to the ones that recharge you and a big X on the ones that deplete you.

If more activities drain than recharge you, strategize ways to change that:

• Who can support you?
• Identify essential but non-urgent tasks.
• Break tasks into monthly or weekly segments to create time for recharging.

"A good teacher is like the rising sun that comes to fill the empty and dark minds with the light of the education"

~ Anamika Mishra

How do you recharge and fill yourself so that you have the capacity to fill your students? Consider how you strive to bring light and enlightenment to your students' "empty and dark minds" through education. In what ways have your students given you light or taught you something new and meaningful?

_____

_____

_____

_____

_____

_____

_____

_____

_____

_____

_____

_____

_____

_____

_____

_____

_____

_____

_____

WHAT DO YOU ENJOY DOING?

So often, when we find the time to do something for ourselves, we face decision paralysis.
Circle everything that you either love to do or want to try.

PHYSICAL ACTIVITIES

Basketball*

Biking

Cornhole*

Crossfit

Fishing

Flag Football*

Frisbee Golf*

Gardening

Golf

Hiking

Hobby Horse Competition*

Ice Skating

Kayaking/Canoeing

Kickball*

Lifting Weights

Pickleball*

Racquetball/Squash

Rafting/Tubing

Rock Climbing

Roller Skating

Running

Soccer*

Softball*

Swimming

Tennis*

Ultimate Frisbee*

Volleyball*

Walking

Yoga

CREATIVE HOBBIES

Building

Calligraphy

Coloring

Cooking

Crocheting/Knitting

Digital Art

Drawing

Embroidery

Flower Arranging Class

Painting

Photography

Playing an Instrument

Pottery

Restoring/Repurposing Furniture

Scrapbooking

Sculpting

Sewing

Theater Performing

RELAXATION & MINDFULNESS

Meditation

People Watching at a Cafe

Picnic

Reading (for fun)

Stargazing

Watching Clouds

Writing

SOCIAL FUN

Art Gallery Gallivanting

Beer/Wine/Distillery Tasting

Comedy Club

Dancing

Festivals

Flea Markets

Food Tours

Attending the Theater

Karaoke

Trivia or Bingo Nights

LEARNING & EXPLORATION

Bird Watching

Camping

Cooking Classes

Escape Room

Genealogy Classes

Language Exchanges

Local History

Magic Classes

Mixology Classes

Music Lessons

Nature Walks

Scavenger Hunt

Traveling

Volunteering

Visiting a Museum

*Indicates activities that are part of adult leagues or organized sports teams, ideal for those who prefer something more structured.

Taking Time to Refresh

List three of the activities you circled that you're passionate about but struggle to find time for.

Commit to engaging in at least one of these activities within the upcoming week.
Schedule the specific day and time in your calendar.

What are the three next steps you need to take to ensure you take time to refresh?

"Education is the most powerful weapon which you can use to change the world."
~ Nelson Mandela

Reflect on the teacher(s) or adult(s) who positively impacted your life in your youth. Write their names on the labels and then list how their influence shaped or directed your path.

HOW CAN YOU HAVE THIS SAME IMPACT ON THE STUDENTS YOU TEACH?

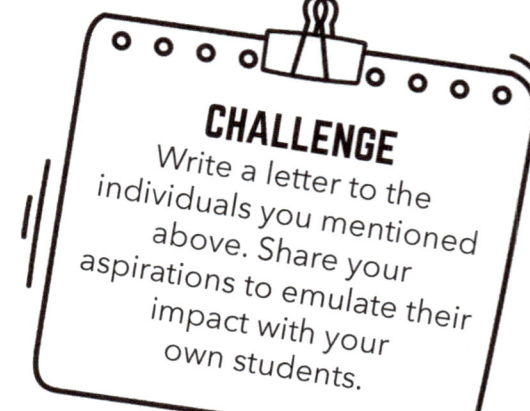

CHALLENGE
Write a letter to the individuals you mentioned above. Share your aspirations to emulate their impact with your own students.

"If you look behind every exceptional person there is an exceptional teacher."

~ Stephen Hawking

What if we were to reverse this and say, "If you look behind every exceptional teacher there is an exceptional person"? What are some of the most exceptional qualities that make you such a loving, passionate, relational, and inspiring teacher? Write them below.

_____

_____

_____

_____

_____

_____

_____

_____

_____

Consider the effort and commitment needed to develop the qualities that make you exceptional as a person and teacher. Write down all the ways to ensure you allocate time to nurture these attributes.

_____

_____

_____

_____

_____

_____

_____

_____

_____

CONTENT CURATOR

SECTION 3

WHAT IS A CONTENT CURATOR?

ESSENTIAL QUESTIONS

How can we determine what content is most relevant and meaningful to our students while maintaining learning objectives?

How can we, as educators, embrace our curiosity and need so that we remain life-long learners?

Curating content ensures the knowledge you are sharing has:
- Depth.
- Relevance.
- Rigor.
- Engagement.
- Motivation.

A teacher as a Content Curator:
- Creates custom learning experiences for students by infusing the curriculum with curiosity.
- Keeps track of trending topics in their field, allowing them to stay up-to-date on new advancements or research and to ensure their students learn through the most up-to-date materials available.

A student as a Content Curator:
- Learns more interactively and develops critical thinking skills.
- Ignites curiosity and encourages lifelong learning.

Imagine walking through a museum, not just on a busy school trip, but in a quiet moment of personal exploration. Consider the impact of that experience, the sights that captivated you, the knowledge you absorbed, and how it made you feel. Why? Every artifact displayed and every interactive piece has been meticulously curated to spark wonder and connection.

The way we decorate our homes and classrooms demonstrates our personalities, interests, and creativity. The items we surround ourselves with weave magic through the use of the art of content curation. It's not just about picking information; it's crafting learning experiences that resonate with us both personally and professionally.

Content is a broad term, representing anything from text to videos to artifacts. For educators, content is the toolbox from which we construct our lessons. The trick lies in selecting resources that are accurate, timely, engaging, and adhere to academic standards, all while piquing both our student's innate curiosity and our own. When we are engaged and motivated, so are our students.

Content isn't just about the what; it's also about the how. When we revise and intertwine this content into a narrative, rich with visuals and multimedia, we capture our students' imaginations.

Refined content curation means:
- Using high-quality sources to ensure impactful lessons.
- Addressing students' needs.
- Allowing for students to explore what they are curious about concerning the subject.

Remember that effective content curation forges an educational odyssey. It's your chance to transform every lesson into a personal museum visit, where each student connects with the wonder of learning. Reflect, engage, and curate—craft an educational narrative as compelling as it is informative. Share the art of content curation with your students and watch their curiosity ignite.

Why is Content Curation Important for Educators Professionally?

Navigating the vast sea of information available in today's digital age can be overwhelming for educators. With so much content at our fingertips, curating accurate, timely, and engaging resources for our students is crucial. Effective content curation helps us find the best resources for our lessons and creates a narrative that captures our students' imagination and sparks their natural inquisitiveness.

By carefully selecting and organizing content for our lessons, we can ensure that students receive high-quality information that meets academic standards. This helps them learn and retain information more effectively and teaches them the importance of discerning between reliable and unreliable sources.

> **Share the art of content curation with your students and watch their curiosity ignite.**

Why is Content Curation Important for Educators Personally?

We can't lose our sense of curiosity. The world is constantly changing, and we must embrace our sense of wonder by telling our story, learning from others, staying up-to-date on current ideas, and remembering why we love learning in the first place. We tend to get lost in the content of our curriculum. Make sure you take time to get lost in the content of your life. What is important to you? What do you want to learn? What brings you joy? Go and learn!

WEEKLY CHECK IN

Choose at least three days this week you will spend doing something creative.

◯ ◯ ◯ ◯ ◯ ◯ ◯

s   m   t   w   t   f   s

This week I am curious about:

1. _____

2. _____

3. _____

Three things I am grateful for:

1. _____

2. _____

3. _____

WEEKLY AFFIRMATION:

CHALLENGE OF THE WEEK

How might I embrace my inner storyteller to curate curiosity?

_____

_____

_____

_____

_____

Personal goals for this week:

_____

_____

_____

_____

Professional goals for this week:

_____

_____

_____

_____

Think about a pencil. We have used pencils since we were children and yet, how much do you know about them?

In one minute, write down all the questions you have regarding a pencil. Ready...go!

Here's the point. **We can't lose our sense of curiosity. The more we wonder, imagine, and question, the deeper we will think and embrace the world around us.**

"You can teach a student a lesson for a day; but if you can teach him to learn by creating curiosity, he will continue the learning process as long as he lives."

~ Clay P. Bedford

When we are curious we are engaged. Reflect on a time when your curiosity was successfully ignited, and it made a lasting impact on your learning journey. Describe the strategies employed to foster your curiosity and engagement. How might you use those techniques or activities to effectively cultivate a culture of lifelong learning among your students? How can you further enhance your teaching practices to inspire curiosity and continuously promote self-directed learning in your students?

_____

_____

_____

_____

_____

_____

_____

_____

_____

_____

_____

_____

_____

_____

_____

_____

If a true education cultivates lifelong learning, which is made up of curiosity, creativity, and passion, what ignites these in you?

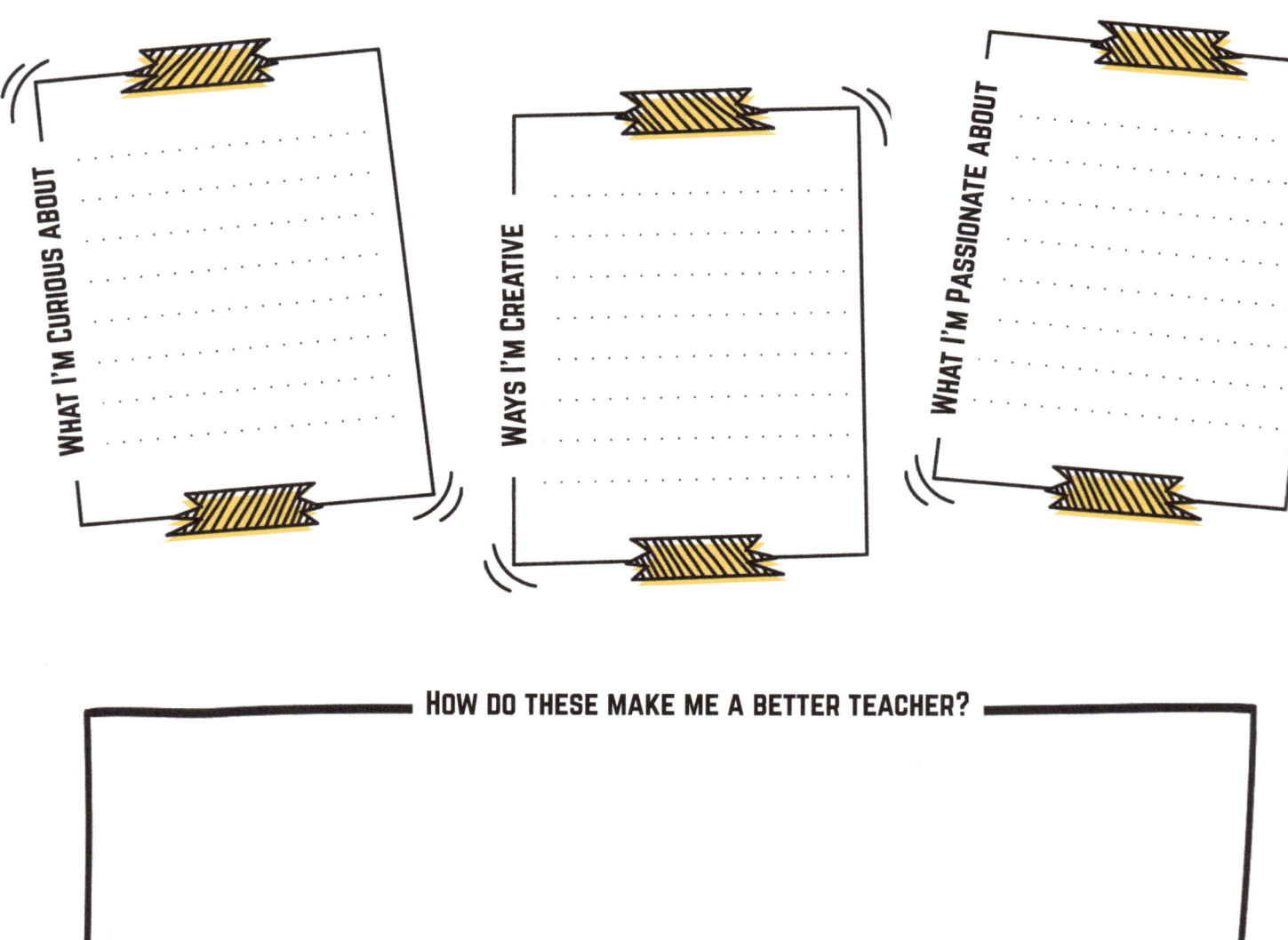

WHAT I'M CURIOUS ABOUT

WAYS I'M CREATIVE

WHAT I'M PASSIONATE ABOUT

HOW DO THESE MAKE ME A BETTER TEACHER?

How has nurturing your own curiosities, passions, and creativity positively influenced your effectiveness in the classroom? What proactive measures can you implement to continue fostering this mindset?

Knowledge is proud that she knows so much; Wisdom is humble that she knows no more.

~ William Cowper

Reflect on the distinction between knowledge and wisdom as described in Cowper's quote. Consider instances in your life where you've encountered individuals who possess vast knowledge but lack humility, as well as those who exhibit wisdom through their humility despite limited knowledge. How do you personally define knowledge and wisdom, and how do they intersect or diverge in your understanding? Reflect on the value of humility in the pursuit of wisdom and the acknowledgment of one's limitations. How can cultivating humility enhance your own journey toward wisdom? Think about how you can apply Cowper's insight to your approach to learning, growth, and interacting with others. Use the image below to record your thoughts.

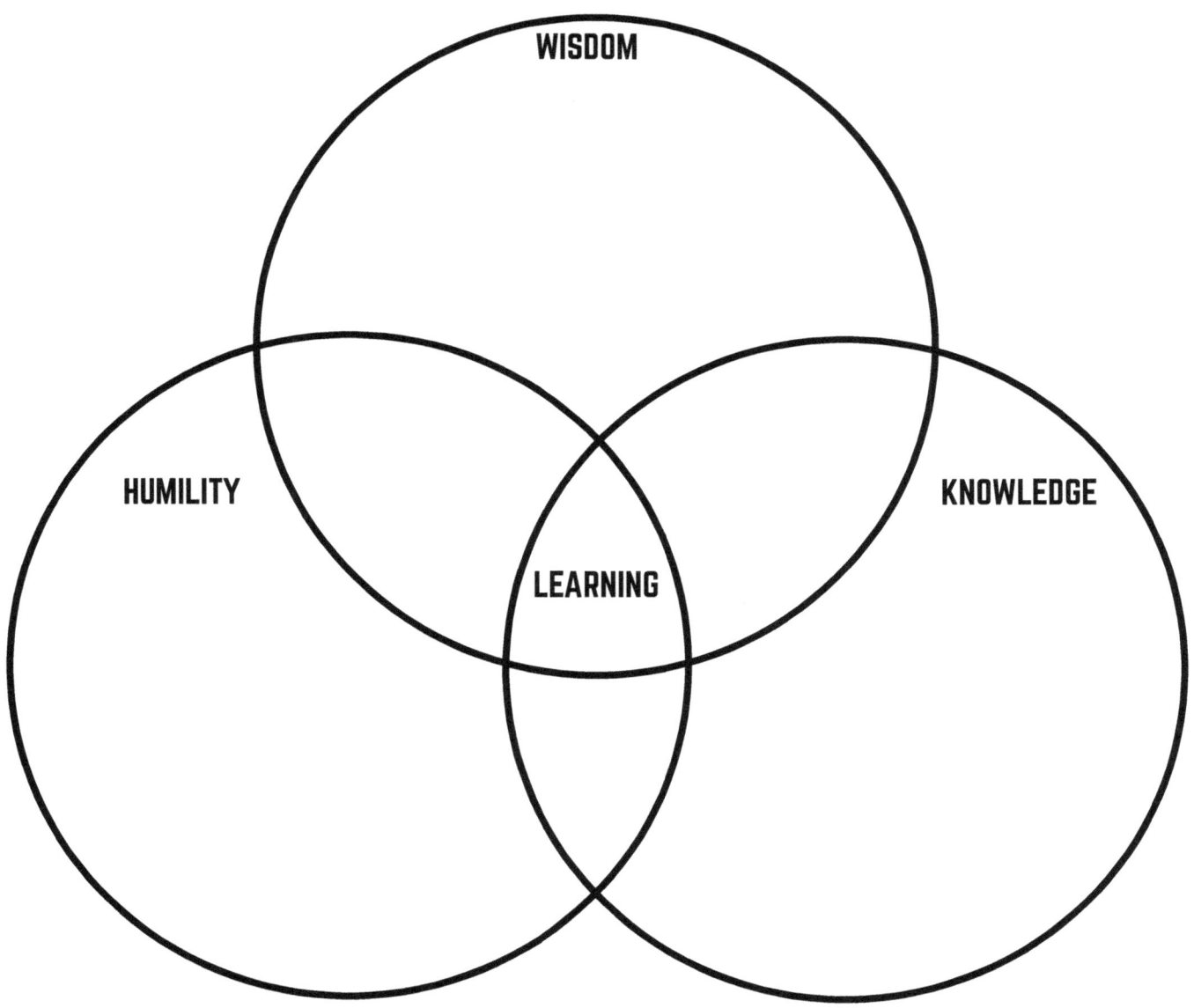

"A well-educated mind will always have more questions than answers."

~ Helen Keller

Reflect on a time when you encountered a question that sparked curiosity or challenged your existing understanding of a topic. How did this question prompt you to delve deeper into your studies or explore new avenues of thought? Consider the role of inquiry in the process of learning and knowledge acquisition. Reflect on Helen Keller's assertion that a well-educated mind tends to generate more questions than answers. What do you think this statement reveals about the nature of education and intellectual growth? How can embracing curiosity and questioning contribute to your own development as a lifelong learner?

_____

_____

_____

_____

_____

_____

_____

_____

_____

_____

_____

_____

_____

_____

_____

_____

CURIOSITY QUESTIONS

Using the questions starters on the right, write deep, challenging questions you can use to cultivate curiosity in your students. It might help to reflect on current students.

Why....?
What are the reasons...?
What if...?
What is the purpose of...?
How would it be different if...?
Suppose that...?
What if we knew...?
What would it change if...?

REFLECT

What steps might you take to instill curiosity as a foundational skill in your classroom?

RISK

FACILITATOR

SECTION 4

WHAT IS A RISK FACILITATOR?

ESSENTIAL QUESTIONS

How can we encourage students to push outside their comfort zone and enter their creative zone?

How can we encourage ourselves to push outside our comfort zones and into our creative zones?

Risk Facilitator emphasizes that sharing knowledge can:
• Be uncomfortable at times.
• Be transformational.
• Be prone to failure.

A teacher as a Risk Facilitator:
• Creates a new and innovative curriculum despite the chance that the lesson could flop.
• Becomes vulnerable with their students regarding their own celebration of failures.
• Believes in themselves and their ability to be creative.

A student as a Risk Facilitator:
• Embraces and celebrates failure.
• Challenges themselves to overcome learning obstacles on their own before asking for help.
• Believes in themselves and their ability to be creative.

To foster academic risk-taking in the classroom:
• Create a safe space for sharing ideas without judgment.
• Implement diverse learning activities that challenge students.
• Emphasize reflection on failures as part of the learning process.

Unlocking students' potential through academic risk-taking is key to shaping their learning experience and empowering them for the future. This approach fosters growth, curiosity, and creativity in a supportive classroom environment.

To create this atmosphere in your classroom:
• Incorporate and practice trust and open communication in your classroom.
• Provide various opportunities for risk-taking.
• Create challenging assignments and creative projects that cater to different learning styles and promote skill development.
• Celebrate efforts and failures.
• Inspire and reward perseverance and resilience in students.
• Lead by example and share how you take risks in your life.

Embracing academic risk-taking isn't just about achievements; it's about instilling a passion for learning and enabling students to contribute meaningfully to society. By encouraging this mindset, educators can boost student confidence and engagement for a lifelong love of education.

Why is Risk Taking Important for Educators Professionally?
Getting stuck in a routine is easy, but taking risks professionally can lead to great rewards. By stepping out of our comfort zones and trying new things, we stay current with innovative teaching methods and build trust and rapport with our students. Embracing failure as a learning opportunity sets a positive climate.

- Start small: Implement a new activity or teaching strategy instead of completely revamping your curriculum.

- Seek support: Talk to other educators in person or online in safe spaces, attend workshops or conferences, and gather ideas from different sources to help you with your risk-taking journey. Join an online community, like the Creative Thinking Network, where you can collaborate with other educators, ask questions, take courses, and find support.

- Reflect on the process: After taking a risk, take some time to reflect on what worked well and what could be improved. Use this feedback to continue growing and learning from your experiences.

Embrace and celebrate failure to unlock creativity.

Why is Risk Taking Important for Educators Personally?
Every risk should have a 'why' that resonates with who we are or aspire to become. This embedded sense of purpose pushes us to endure when times grow tough. Finding this 'why' may require that we take risks, especially in times of uncertainty, and can cause criticism and second-guessing when the path ahead dims.

To grow, one must be resilient, weather the storms of uncertainty, and sometimes falter before re-emerging with renewed determination. In taking risks, we test our determination, affirming that although we are imperfect humans, we can overcome anything. Through this process, our confidence grows, leaving us stronger, both mentally and physically.

Remember, fostering academic risk-taking is an ongoing effort that requires dedication from both educators and students. The rewards are substantial. They are confident learners who embrace challenges and significantly impact the world.

WEEKLY CHECK IN

Choose at least three days this week you will spend doing something creative.

○ ○ ○ ○ ○ ○ ○
s   m   t   w   t   f   s

This week I'm going to focus on creativity by:

1. _____

2. _____

3. _____

Three things I am grateful for:

1. _____

2. _____

3. _____

WEEKLY AFFIRMATION:

CHALLENGE OF THE WEEK

How might I celebrate failure in my personal life?

_____

_____

_____

_____

_____

Personal goals for this week:

_____

_____

_____

_____

Professional goals for this week:

_____

_____

_____

_____

How has embracing uncertainty led you to unexpected adventures through risk-taking? Write your ideas in the road.

HOW CAN YOUR EXPERIENCES INSPIRE STUDENTS TO EMBRACE ADVENTURE IN UNCERTAINTY?

"Knowledge is an unending adventure at the edge of uncertainty."
~ Jacob Bronowski

How does your perspective on risk-taking and uncertainty align with the assertion that knowledge is an ongoing adventure? How does this perspective influence your approach to life, teaching, and learning?

_____

_____

_____

_____

_____

_____

_____

_____

_____

_____

_____

_____

_____

_____

_____

_____

_____

Curiosity Thrives Where Failure Begins

What does celebrating failure look like in the classroom? Failure has become a taboo word, not just for students but also for parents, administrators, and teachers. Fear of failure is real, and many times, it causes self-doubt and anxiety.

Often, students will choose not to participate out of fear of being wrong, and therefore, judged by their peers and teachers. Offering opportunities to celebrate failure and to embrace it as a learning experience is vital as we build trusting relationships with our students and inspire them to take academic risks.

Feedback is a key component to embracing failure. If students know they can fail and it will not negatively impact their grades, they will be likelier to try something new.

F	A	I	L	S
FREEDOM	**ATTITUDE**	**INDIVIDUALITY**	**LEARNING**	**STRENGTHS**
Failure in the classroom can liberate students from the fear of making mistakes. It teaches them it's okay to fail and failure is a part of the learning process.	Encountering failure can change a student's attitude toward learning by making them understand that it's not just about getting the right answers but also about learning.	Failure can encourage students to find their unique ways of understanding and solving problems, fostering individuality.	Failure serves as a powerful tool for invoking deep learning as it forces students to analyze their mistakes and understand where they went wrong.	Failure can help students identify their strengths as they navigate challenges and find ways to overcome them.

Consider your own personal or professional failures. What are some lessons have you learned?

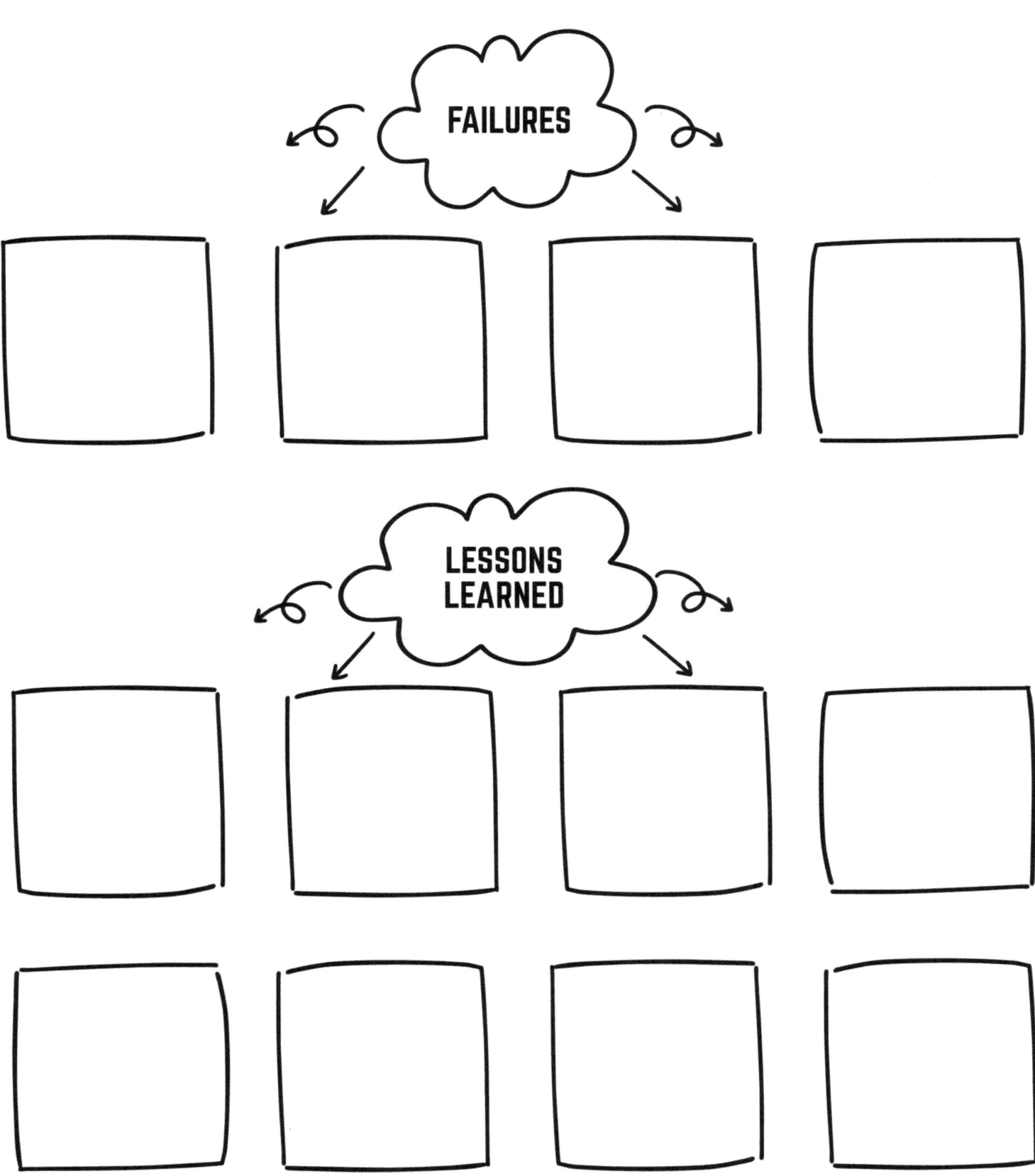

"There is no innovation and creativity without failure."

~ Brené Brown

Fail is seen as a four letter word. Our students fear it instead of celebrating it. Even as educators, we often fear making mistakes in front of administrators or our students. Yet, without failure, we cannot truly learn and grow. Failure is a natural part of the learning process. It allows us to identify areas for improvement and gain valuable experience. However, our society tends to view failure as a negative outcome rather than an opportunity for growth.

As educators, we need to shift this mindset among our students. Instead of fearing failure, we should encourage our students to embrace it as a necessary step towards success. This can be done by creating a safe and supportive environment where making mistakes is seen as a normal and essential part of the learning process.

How is failure viewed in your classroom? How do you know?
How might you create more opportunities to celebrate failure?

_____

_____

_____

_____

_____

_____

_____

_____

_____

_____

_____

_____

_____

It's often easier to recall our biggest mistakes than it is our greatest successes.
List the personal or professional mistakes you still struggle to let go of.
Then, fill in every square with successes you are proud of.

MISTAKES

SUCCESSES

"Self-awareness gives you the capacity to learn from your mistakes as well as your successes."
~ Lawrence Bossidy

Looking back, what is one mistake (large or small) you have made (personally or professionally) and what did you learn from it?

What impact did that mistake make on you?

_____

_____

_____

_____

_____

_____

_____

_____

_____

_____

_____

_____

_____

_____

_____

BEING A RISK TAKER MEANS...
EMBRACING PRODUCTIVE STRUGGLE

What is productive struggle?

Unlocking student potential with productive struggle in the classroom is all about embracing challenges to promote growth and learning. By presenting tasks that push students to think critically, providing support when needed, and encouraging perseverance in the face of setbacks, teachers create an environment where students can thrive.

Key aspects of productive struggle include:

- Challenge: Tasks that require critical thinking and application of knowledge.

- Support: Guidance and resources to navigate challenges.

- Perseverance: Encouragement to keep going and learn from mistakes.

- Reflection: Opportunities to analyze thinking processes and problem-solving strategies.

- Autonomy: Empowering students to take charge of their learning journey.

Productive struggle not only enhances critical thinking skills but also builds confidence and resilience. It's a recipe for creating independent learners who aren't afraid to tackle complex problems head-on. Teachers play a crucial role in finding the right balance of challenge and support to keep students engaged and motivated throughout their learning journey.

WEEKLY CHECK IN

Choose at least three days this week you will spend doing something creative.

○ ○ ○ ○ ○ ○ ○
s m t w t f s

This week I'm going to focus on being a risk facilitator by:

1. _____

2. _____

3. _____

Three things I am grateful for:

1. _____

2. _____

3. _____

WEEKLY AFFIRMATION:

CHALLENGE OF THE WEEK

What might be all the things that I need to push through the struggle to finish?

_____

_____

_____

_____

_____

Personal goals for this week:

_____

_____

_____

Professional goals for this week:

_____

_____

_____

Take a look at the kettlebells below. What are your biggest challenges at home and at school? Rate them by their mental weight. How might you change them into passions?

HOME

SCHOOL

*"Hard work spotlights the character of people: some turn up their sleeves,
some turn up their noses, and some don't turn up at all."*

~ Sam Ewing

How would you define your personal work ethic? Is it something you were taught? Inherited? When you were the age of your current students, was your view of hard work different? How is work completed today compared to when you were a student? How might you foster a culture of hard work and perseverance in your classroom to help all students thrive?

_____

_____

_____

_____

_____

_____

_____

_____

_____

_____

_____

_____

_____

_____

_____

_____

Why, What's Stopping You?

When you are engaged in a struggle, it helps to understand your feelings relating to it and what might be holding you back from fixing it. We can, after all, be our own worst impediments.

1 Write your challenge in the box.

2 Next, write ALL the reasons why you want to solve it.

3 Now write ALL the things that are stopping you. Phrase these as open ended questions. You can start them with "How to…" or "What might be all the ways…"

4 Finally, write how you can overcome those things that are stopping you.

"When everything seems to be going against you, remember that the airplane takes off against the wind, not with it."

~ Henry Ford

Write about a time when you faced significant challenges or setbacks personally or professionally. How did you navigate through that adversity?
Reflect on Henry Ford's analogy of the airplane taking off against the wind.
How can you apply this perspective to overcome obstacles in your life?

_____

_____

_____

_____

_____

_____

_____

_____

_____

_____

_____

_____

_____

_____

_____

_____

_____

Reflect on your significant struggles. What lessons did you learn? What new approaches could you use to try to turn those experiences into successes, whether personally or professionally?

LESSONS LEARNED · LESSONS LEARNED · LESSONS LEARNED · LESSONS LEARNED · LESSONS LEARNED · LESSONS LEARNED · LESSONS LEARNED

WHAT MINDSET SHIFT DO YOU NEED TO SEE STRUGGLES AS OPPORTUNITIES FOR NEW GROWTH RATHER THAN AS DEFINING YOUR CAPABILITIES?

"I can accept failure. Everybody fails at something.
But I can't accept not trying. Fear is an illusion."

~ Michael Jordan

Reflect on a moment when you faced fear or the possibility of failure. How did you navigate through that fear or uncertainty? Reflect on how Michael Jordan's perseverance resonates with your own experiences in life or the classroom. How can embracing the idea that "fear is an illusion" influence your approach to teaching and learning through struggling?

_____

_____

_____

_____

_____

_____

_____

_____

_____

_____

_____

_____

_____

_____

_____

_____

EXPERIENCE
NAVIGATOR

SECTION 5

WHAT IS AN EXPERIENCE NAVIGATOR?

ESSENTIAL QUESTIONS

How can we make the learning experience meaningful, relevant, and beneficial for all students?

How can I continue to make my personal learning experience meaningful, relevant and beneficial to my life mission?

An Experience Navigator ensures knowledge is shared in a way that is:
- Relevant.
- Meaningful.
- Engaging.
- Challenging.

A teacher as an Experience Navigator:
- Creates a curriculum that allows students to experience the study material differently.
- Becomes a tour guide, allowing students to create personalized learning experiences.
- Embraces challenging and ambiguous classroom moments.

> Curiosity and open-mindedness are essential for growth and development in experience-driven classrooms.

A student as an Experience Navigator:
- Embraces and celebrates ambiguity.
- Challenges themselves to look at learning as a creative and personalized experience.
- Believes in themselves enough to take control of their own learning experience and know when to ask for guidance.

Experience Navigators cultivate a classroom where creativity thrives.

It looks like:

- Student's unique strengths are embraced in an interactive learning environment that encourages curiosity and active participation.

- Students are empowered to take charge of their education, sparking a drive to discover and innovate beyond the traditional classroom setting.

- The classroom focuses on experiences and nurtures creativity and independence.

- Every child e mbraces their unique strengths and interests and begins to develop those strengths and explore their passions.

- Learning environments are designed to engage students in critical thinking, problem-solving, and collaboration.

- Learning is not a passive experience but rather an active and dynamic process where student can explore and experiment with different ideas.

In classrooms where experience navigators thrive, curiosity and open-mindedness is encouraged and asking questions and seeking answers is essential for growth and development. Teachers act as facilitators, guiding students toward finding their own answers and fostering a love for learning, empowering students to take charge of their education. By giving them ownership over their learning, we promote independence, self-motivation, and self-discovery, creating a sense of responsibility and achievement within each student.

Why is it important to be an Experience Navigator professionally?
By incorporating real-world experiences and projects into the curriculum, students see the practical applications of their learning, inspiring them to think deeper and innovate. Strive to create an environment where students can thrive both academically and personally. As educators, we aim to equip our students with the skills, knowledge, and values necessary to become confident, creative, and independent individuals ready to navigate their own paths toward success.

Why is it important to be an Experience Navigator personally?
Teachers have a heart for education and learning, yet often, we need to remember to take the time to enrich our knowledge with meaningful experiences. When we invest in our personal learning experiences we invest in ourselves. Is there a DIY project you want to start? A part of history you want to explore? A trip you want to want to plan? Start navigating your own experiences.

WEEKLY CHECK IN

Choose at least three days this week you will spend doing something creative.

◯ ◯ ◯ ◯ ◯ ◯ ◯
s   m   t   w   t   f   s

This week I'm going to focus on my personal learning by:

1. _____

2. _____

3. _____

Three things I am grateful for:

1. _____

2. _____

3. _____

WEEKLY AFFIRMATION:

CHALLENGE OF THE WEEK

What might be all the ways I can use my experiences this week to enhance my learning?

_____

_____

_____

_____

_____

Personal goals for this week:

_____

_____

_____

Professional goals for this week:

_____

_____

_____

As educators, we often overlook the importance of nurturing our creativity. How can you prioritize purposeful play in your personal life? List various ways to nurture your creativity, starting with those you are most likely to implement.

PRIORITIZE CREATIVITY

☐ _____

☐ _____

☐ _____

☐ _____

☐ _____

☐ _____

☐ _____

☐ _____

☐ _____

☐ _____

☐ _____

☐ _____

☐ _____

☐ _____

☐ _____

How does focusing on personal creativity carry over to you enjoying your job more?

"Life can only be understood backwards;
but it must be lived forwards."

~ Soren Kierkegaard

Balancing forward momentum with retrospective reflection is crucial in life. How do you navigate between actively engaging in experiences and setting aside time for reflective introspection?

_____

_____

_____

_____

_____

_____

_____

_____

_____

_____

_____

_____

_____

_____

_____

_____

Navigating an experience includes debriefing what happened and how it went.
Here is a great format that you can use personally and in the classroom.
Try it! Reflect on recent experiences and complete the following chart.

NEW THINGS I DO WELL		NEW THINGS I DO NOT DO WELL	
FAVORITE THINGS I DO WELL		**FAVORITE THINGS I DO NOT DO WELL**	
I HAVE A TALENT	I NEED PRACTICE	I CAN HELP OTHERS WITH	I NEED HELP WITH

What are some next steps you can take to move the items in the right column, to the left column.?

(This is from a Doug Fisher lecture given at the 2024 Learning and the Brain conference.)

*"One must learn by doing the thing; for though you think you know it,
you have no certainty, until you try."*

~ Sophocles

Consider moments where hands-on learning or experiential activities have proven more effective than traditional methods with you as the learner and with your students. How did your or their understanding evolve through the process of "learning by doing?"

_____

_____

_____

_____

_____

_____

_____

_____

_____

_____

_____

_____

_____

_____

_____

_____

John Dewey said "Give the pupils something to do, not something to learn; and the doing is of such a nature as to demand thinking; learning naturally results."

Experience comes through DOING.

TODAY

- [ ]
- [ ]
- [ ]
- [ ]
- [ ]
- [ ]

NEXT WEEK

- [ ]
- [ ]
- [ ]
- [ ]
- [ ]

NEXT DECADE

- [ ]
- [ ]
- [ ]
- [ ]
- [ ]
- [ ]
- [ ]
- [ ]
- [ ]
- [ ]
- [ ]
- [ ]
- [ ]
- [ ]

NEXT MONTH

- [ ]
- [ ]
- [ ]
- [ ]
- [ ]
- [ ]

NEXT YEAR

- [ ]
- [ ]
- [ ]
- [ ]
- [ ]

START YOUR LIST THEN CREATE YOUR PLAN

*"The purpose of life is to live it, to taste experience to the utmost,
to reach out eagerly and without fear for newer and richer experience."*

~ Eleanor Roosevelt

How has your eagerness to explore and experience enriched your life? How can you foster a classroom environment that encourages students to "taste experience to the utmost" and embrace new opportunities for growth and learning? How do you cultivate these qualities in your students, allowing them to reach out eagerly for newer and richer experiences?

_____

_____

_____

_____

_____

_____

_____

_____

_____

_____

_____

_____

_____

_____

_____

_____

_____

_____

ATTITUDE

SHIFTER

SECTION 6

WHAT IS AN ATTITUDE SHIFTER?

ESSENTIAL QUESTIONS

How can we teach open-mindedness and acceptance while embracing differing perspectives?

How can I learn to embrace open-mindedness and acceptance while embracing differing perspectives?

Attitude shifting ensures knowledge is shared in a way that promotes:

- Belonging.
- Purpose.
- Compassion.
- Open-mindedness.

Strategies we will examine are:

- Dealing with ambiguity.
- Purpose-driven learning.
- Reflection versus mindset.

Attitude Shifter includes:

- Being open to new ideas and perspectives.
- Deferring judgment.
- Listening with an open mind.
- Being vulnerable with others.
- Reflecting on how and why you feel the way you do.
- Taking responsibility for one's attitude toward different situations.

Education is a lifelong journey that nourishes curiosity and creativity.

A teacher as an Attitude Shifter:

- Creates a curriculum that allows students to reflect on different perspectives while keeping an open mind.
- Becomes a facilitator, allowing students to debate, listen, and research with compassion, empathy, and purpose.
- Challenges students to reflect on what they have learned and their attitude toward the learning process.

A student as an Attitude Shifter:
- Embraces and celebrates different perspectives.
- Challenges themselves to be open-minded and empathetic toward ideas that may differ from theirs.
- Demonstrates confidence even when the material being presented may be complex and make them feel uncomfortable at times.

Attitude Shifter redefines education as a lifelong, engaging process that nourishes curiosity and creativity rather than just a pathway to grades and jobs. It encourages a mindset shift towards viewing the classroom as a realm for explorative adventures and personal growth. The core of Attitude Shifter involves openness to fresh ideas, deferment of judgment, active and empathetic listening, and a vulnerability that inspires reflection and personal responsibility in learning attitudes.

For educators, embodying an Attitude Shifter means crafting lessons that foster open-mindedness and a purpose-driven environment, promoting a sense of belonging and encouraging students to consider diverse perspectives. By facilitating discussions and debates with compassion, teachers can help students understand the impact of their learning and their own attitudes toward it.

Embracing Attitude Shifting will:
- Incorporate real-world experiences and hands-on learning opportunities that help bridge the gap between traditional education and real-life applications.
- Celebrate varying viewpoints.
- Challenge limits of acceptance.
- Build confidence when confronting complex materials.
- Help students develop critical thinking skills and problem-solving abilities.
- Unlock the full potential of education as a transformative tool.
- Encourages a growth mindset.
- Promote creativity and curiosity.
- Cultivate empathy and open-mindedness.

With this mindset shift, education can become more than just a means to an end but a lifelong journey of personal growth and development.

Why is Attitude Shifter important professionally?
Imagine a classroom where you and your students create an educational experience that is fruitful, relevant, and ultimately transformative. To fully embrace the Attitude Shifter mindset, incorporate certain practices into your daily classroom routines, such as practicing gratitude and mindfulness, engaging in self-reflection exercises, and actively seeking diverse perspectives through reading and discussions. Your classroom will become a safe place for students to collaborate and communicate. The rapport and sense of community inside your four walls will be one you and your students will value and embrace.

Why is Attitude Shifter important personally?
The teacher's lounge can be a place of positivity or a place of toxic negative attitudes. Being an Attitude Shifter is important personally because it allows us, as educators, to take control of our own mindset and create a positive environment for ourselves, coworkers, family, and friends. It empowers us to break away from negative attitudes and embrace a mindset that promotes an environment we enjoy and thrive in. We can carry a lot of baggage home with us: stress, anxiety, worry, and frustration. We must make a concerted effort to shift our attitudes to find peace and contentment to be present for our family, friends, and ourselves.

WEEKLY CHECK IN

Choose at least three days this week you will spend doing something creative.

◯ ◯ ◯ ◯ ◯ ◯ ◯
s   m   t   w   t   f   s

This week I'm going to focus on being an attitude shifter by:

1. _____

2. _____

3. _____

Three things I am grateful for:

1. _____

2. _____

3. _____

WEEKLY AFFIRMATION:

CHALLENGE OF THE WEEK

How might I ensure my attitude this week is focused on what I can do and control?

_____

_____

_____

_____

_____

Personal goals for this week:

_____

_____

_____

Professional goals for this week:

_____

_____

_____

"The best thing about being a teacher is that it matters. The hardest thing about being a teacher is that it matters every day.

~ Todd Whitaker

Contemplate the immense impact teachers have on their students' lives and the sense of purpose derived from knowing that your work truly matters. How do you navigate the complexities of teaching while maintaining your passion and dedication? How do you find balance between the rewarding moments of impact and the ongoing demands of the job?

_____

_____

_____

_____

_____

_____

_____

_____

_____

_____

_____

_____

_____

_____

_____

_____

_____

Thoughts I've been holding on to that I need to get out

When our brain is "filled" with ideas, it can "use up" thought space and make us tired and less focused. Writing these thoughts down helps release them from our brain, and it is then free to think of other things.

"Men build too many walls and not enough bridges."

~ Joseph Fort Newton

Reflect on the role of empathy in your personal life. How do you strive to understand and connect with the diverse experiences, perspectives, and emotions of others?
How does this quote resonate with your understanding of empathy in teaching and learning? Consider the importance of building connections and understanding between students, educators, and the broader community.

_____

_____

_____

_____

_____

_____

_____

_____

_____

_____

_____

_____

_____

_____

_____

_____

_____

"It is a narrow mind which cannot look at a subject from various points of view."

~ George Eliot

LEARNING FROM THE PAST

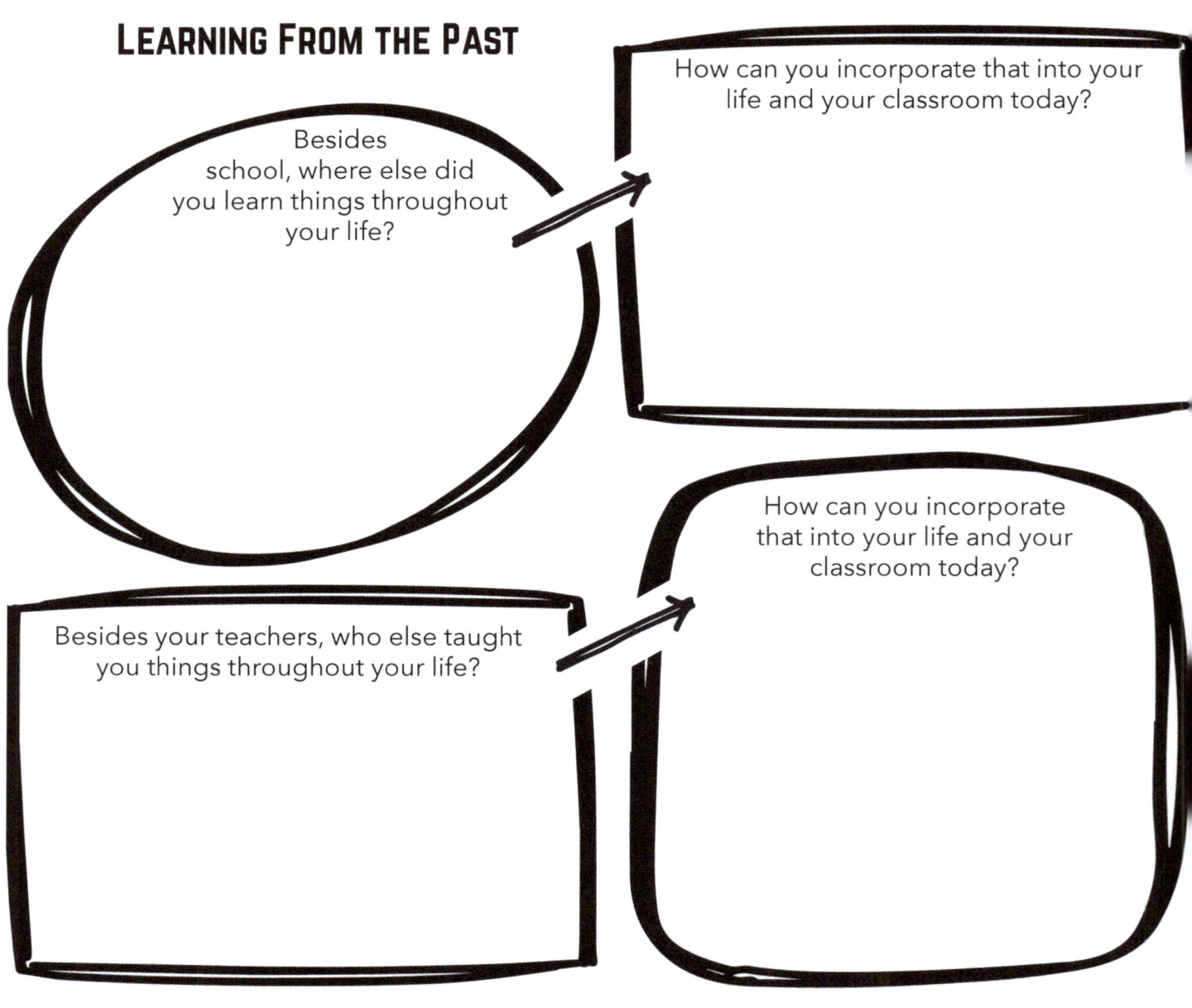

Besides school, where else did you learn things throughout your life?

How can you incorporate that into your life and your classroom today?

Besides your teachers, who else taught you things throughout your life?

How can you incorporate that into your life and your classroom today?

How has narrow-mindedness impacted your relationships or friendships in the past? How could it have been different if there had been openness and receptivity to different perspectives? How do you incorporate opportunities for students to engage with multiple viewpoints and perspectives in your lessons?

_____

_____

_____

_____

"Courage doesn't always roar. Sometimes courage is the quiet voice at the end of the day saying, "I will try again tomorrow."

~ Mary Anne Radmacher

Consider the importance of perseverance and optimism in overcoming challenges and setbacks personally and professionally. How have you had to draw upon your inner courage and positivity to navigate through the challenges and continue moving forward? Reflect on the role of self-talk and mindset in maintaining a positive attitude as an educator. How do you cultivate a mindset of optimism and resilience, even in the face of adversity?

"It is a narrow mind which cannot look at a subject from various points of view."

~ George Eliot

Write down all the things you love about teaching and being a teacher.

Reflect on times in your teaching career when your passion for teaching sparked a love for learning in your students. What might be all the memories that you can tap into on challenging days when teaching feels less joyful?

_____

_____

_____

_____

_____

TEAM TRANSFORMER

SECTION 7

WHAT IS A TEAM TRANSFORMER?

ESSENTIAL QUESTIONS

How can we build strong, creative, collaborative teams with contagious energy?

What are all the ways that I can ensure and encourage good communication in my life and classroom?

The Team Transformer strives to share knowledge in a manner that:
- Actively Listens.
- Celebrates differences.
- Builds on other's strengths.

Team Transformer includes:
- Embracing the ability to be a close listener.
- Exhibiting patience while deferring judgment.
- Capitalizing on one's strengths while revising one's weakness.

Team-based learning cultivates future leaders and global citizens.

A teacher as a Team Transformer:
- Creates a curriculum that challenges students to embrace their weaknesses and share their strengths.
- Becomes a mentor, showing students how to work with people from diverse backgrounds.
- Challenges students to take various roles, at times being a leader and at times the follower.

A student as a Team Transformer:
- Embraces and celebrates the differences in their peers.
- Challenges themselves to be open-minded and empathetic toward their teammates.
- Demonstrates the ability to lead and also the ability to listen.

The education landscape is transitioning towards a focus on teamwork and collaboration, preparing students to thrive in group settings that reflect real-world work environments. In this progressive approach, teachers shift from traditional roles to become facilitators who guide students in leveraging their unique strengths to serve the community.

In a classroom that values team-based learning, individual talents and perspectives inspire creativity and a deep sense of curiosity among students. This dynamic creates a fertile environment for innovative problem-solving and elevates the learning process to an engaging and rewarding experience.

What does a team-based learning classroom look like?

- It is an integrated entity that relies on the synergy of diverse skills to achieve a collective goal.
- Through this collaborative effort—similar to a sports team aiming for a win—students experience the significance of unity and interdependence.
- Learning cultivates critical social and emotional competencies, such as effective communication, negotiation, and empathetic listening.
- It promotes critical thinking, accountability, and a willingness to consider different viewpoints.
- Students are leaders, thinkers, and team players vital for success in a rapidly evolving world.
- Students' collaboration, critical thinking, and social and emotional competencies.
- Academic growth and essential skills for success in the real world are cultivated.

As educators continue to embrace team-based learning, it's crucial to prioritize intentional implementation and assessment methods to realize its full potential. With a strong emphasis on teamwork and community building, team-based learning can truly transform education and equip students with the necessary skills for a bright future. So, it's clear that team-based learning is not just a teaching method but a powerful tool for shaping future leaders and global citizens.

Why is being a Team Transformer important professionally?

Professional Learning Communities are quickly becoming a staple in many schools worldwide. Educators are taking time to work as teams, collaborate on curriculum assessments, and creatively problem-solve behavioral issues. There is great power when educators come together and work towards a common goal. Educators, if given a voice, could transform the educational system as a team.

Why is being a Team Transformer important personally?

Families and friends are teams. We all have different strengths, and when we accept and build on these strengths, much can be accomplished. By incorporating Team Transformer skills into our personal lives, we can surround ourselves with thriving and creative communities that show empathy, actively listen, and embrace different perspectives.

WEEKLY CHECK IN

Choose at least three days this week you will spend doing something creative.

◯ ◯ ◯ ◯ ◯ ◯ ◯
s m t w t f s

This week I'm going to focus on ways I can bring contagious energy to my team by:

1. _____

2. _____

3. _____

Three things I am grateful for:

1. _____

2. _____

3. _____

WEEKLY AFFIRMATION:

CHALLENGE OF THE WEEK

How can I rely on someone else's strengths in an area where I'm weak?

_____

_____

_____

_____

_____

Personal goals for this week:

_____

_____

_____

Professional goals for this week:

_____

_____

_____

GROUP DOODLES

This is meant to be a group activity, but you can do it alone here also.
Add on to these doodles. Invite others to build on what you've drawn, or come back later and add again. Keep going until you have reached the point of ridiculousness.

"It is one of the beautiful compensations of this life that no one can sincerely try to help another without helping himself."

~ Ralph Waldo Emerson

Think about a time when you've experienced the benefits of teamwork and collaboration personally or professionally. How did working together to support one another ultimately benefit the entire team or community? Consider the importance of fostering a culture of teamwork and mutual support with your colleagues and students. How can you cultivate an environment where everyone feels valued, supported, and empowered to contribute to the collective success of the team?

_____

_____

_____

_____

_____

_____

_____

_____

_____

_____

_____

_____

_____

_____

_____

_____

_____

MY VALUES

Write all of your values here.

MY INTERPERSONAL SKILLS

Now write all your strengths in interacting and relating well with others here.

How can you recognize and value others' strengths?
How does combining everyone's values benefit the group as a whole?

"A candle loses nothing of its light when lighting another."
~ Kahlil Gibran

Reflect on the concept of the abundance mentality. How does adopting a mindset of abundance, where there is enough knowledge, support, and success to go around, enhance collaboration and teamwork either personally or professionally? Consider the continued effect of your actions as an educator. How does empowering and supporting your colleagues and students ultimately contribute to a more positive and thriving community?

_____

_____

_____

_____

_____

_____

_____

_____

_____

_____

_____

_____

_____

_____

_____

_____

_____

LISTENING REALLY HARD

Most people think they are good listeners, yet we hardly practice this skill, and it shows.
Take some time to WORK at it. Go outside--in the city or the country,
or anywhere in between and focus on what you HEAR.

Listen for animals

Listen for car sounds

Listen for people sounds

Listen for nature sounds

Listen for insects

Listen for other sounds

Record what you hear and experience.

_____

_____

_____

_____

_____

_____

_____

_____

Write down all of the things that make a good teammate.
Circle the top five you want to work on personally or professionally.

Which three do you want to focus on in your classroom?

1. _____

2. _____

3. _____

EMPATHY MAP

1. WHO ARE WE EMPATHIZING WITH?
- Who is the person we want to understand?
- What is the situation they are in?
- What is their role in the situation?

2. WHAT DO THEY SEE?
What do they see others saying and doing?

6. WHAT DO THEY THINK AND FEEL?
What are their fears, frustrations, and anxieties?

What are their wants, needs, hopes, and dreams?

5. WHAT DO THEY HEAR?
What do they hear others say?

What do they hear from friends?

What do they hear from family?

What do they hear second-hand?

3. WHAT DO THEY SAY?
What have you heard them say? What does this reflect about their perspective/feelings/opinions?

4. WHAT DO THEY DO?
What have they do?

What behavior have you observed?

What does this reflect about their perspective/feelings/opinions?

"None of us, including me, ever do great things. But we can all do small things, with great love, and together we can do something wonderful."

~ Saint Mother Teresa

How does this resonate with your understanding of the impact of small acts of kindness and collaboration with others? Consider how even the smallest gestures of support and compassion can contribute to creating a positive and nurturing environment. Think about a time when you've witnessed the collective power of small acts of kindness or collaboration among educators. How did coming together to support one another and your students lead to something wonderful or transformative within your educational community?
How can you nurture this same culture amongst your students?

_____

_____

_____

_____

_____

_____

_____

_____

_____

_____

_____

_____

_____

_____

_____

_____

_____

WHAT IS AN EVALUATION DESIGNER?

ESSENTIAL QUESTIONS

How can we encourage curiosity and creativity so students can manage, monitor, and modify their own learning?

How can I embrace curiosity and creativity to manage, monitor, and modify my personal learning?

An Evaluation Designer creates methods that assess:
- Motivation and curiosity.
- Different modes of creative thinking.
- Student voice.

Evaluation design includes:
- Clearly defining how different skills will be achieved.
- Being open to various evaluation methods.
- Responsibility and ownership over products presented.

A teacher as an Evaluation Designer:
- Creates assessments that allow feedback.
- Inspires students to self-monitor, self-regulate, and self-modify.
- Challenges students to take on various roles—at times, being leaders and followers.

A student as an Evaluation Designer:
- Discovers different ways to monitor personal growth effectively.
- Pushes themselves and their peers to revise work by offering solid feedback.
- Demonstrates the ability to evaluate the effectiveness of learning honestly.

In the education sector, Evaluation Designers play a pivotal role in measuring student learning by utilizing diverse assessment strategies. Moving away from conventional memorization-focused tests, they underscore the necessity for evaluations that actively involve students as participants in their educational process. By acknowledging each student's unique talents and perspectives, designers tailor assessment experiences to individual needs.

What do Evaluation Designers do?

- Facilitate student expression of both strengths and potential areas for growth.
- Vary evaluation methods to allow students to demonstrate their capabilities in different formats, such as oral presentations or practical applications.
- Craft scenarios that stimulate creative and analytical thinking, encouraging learners to veer off traditional paths.
- Provide feedback that aids students in recognizing their aptitudes and challenges, encouraging them to pursue personal academic excellence.
- Lead students toward showing proficiency in various contexts, transforming them into innovative and evaluative thinkers.
- Shift the focus from a predetermined endpoint to holistic student development.
- Continually adapt practices to meet the ever-changing needs of students.
- Collaborate with other education professionals, attend workshops and conferences, and continuously seek innovative ways to assess student learning.
- Play a significant role in promoting equitable education for all students.

Evaluation Designers transform assessments into tools for innovation.

Thus, evaluation experiences are designed to measure student learning and encourage a positive attitude toward continuous academic and personal improvement. Learning how to manage, monitor, and modify learning is a vital skill needed now and in the future.

Why is being an Evaluation Designer important professionally?
We know that to prepare our students for the future best, they must be innovation-ready, meaning they must know how to think for themselves, adapt to new situations, and cope with ambiguity. By creating evaluations that encourage deeper thinking, problem-solving, and choice and account for multiple current answers, we provide opportunities for students to take ownership of their learning. Professionally, we provide feedback and act as guides while students begin to manage their learning now and in the future.

Why is being an Evaluation Designer important personally?
We can be tough on ourselves. We want the best for ourselves, our students, and our families. We need to take the time to reflect on our learning and accomplishments. Give ourselves a break. Find a mentor. Take a day and read a book. Manage, monitor, and modify our sense of learning. You work hard. You deserve to give yourself an A+.

WEEKLY CHECK IN

Choose at least three days this week you will spend doing something creative.

◯ ◯ ◯ ◯ ◯ ◯ ◯
s   m   t   w   t   f   s

This week I'm going to focus on ways to encourage curiosity in my own learning:

1. _____

2. _____

3. _____

Three things I am grateful for:

1. _____

2. _____

3. _____

WEEKLY AFFIRMATION:

CHALLENGE OF THE WEEK

Have a conversation with other teachers and ask them about their favorite alternative assessments. How might you adjust them to work for your class?

_____

_____

_____

_____

Personal goals for this week:

_____

_____

_____

Professional goals for this week:

_____

_____

_____

The Four I's
An Evaluative Tool

Using this format, evaluate a current problem you are facing personally or professionally. Then take a moment to reflect and take any action you deem needed. Feel free to use this again and again, when dealing with challenges or when you feel overwhelmed.

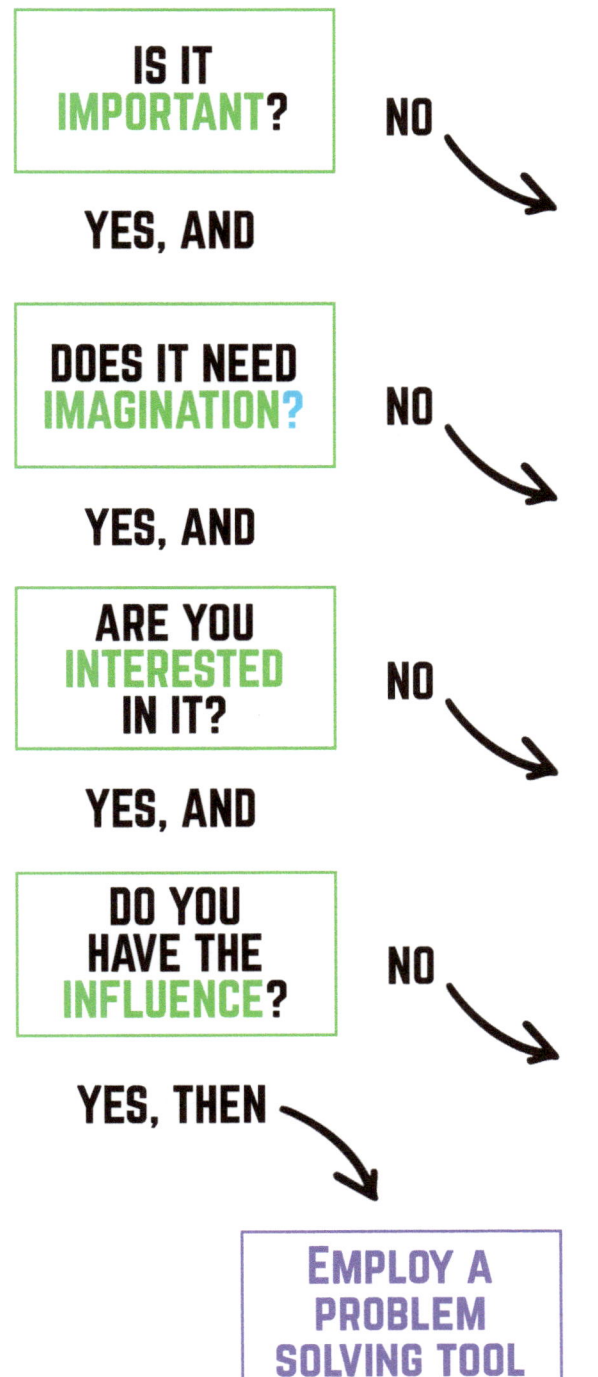

IS IT IMPORTANT?

NO → Then stop what you are doing: you can spend time on other things, or wait until it IS important.

YES, AND

DOES IT NEED IMAGINATION?

NO → This is a to-do list item. Put it on a calendar, get the people's help that you need, and get it done.

YES, AND

ARE YOU INTERESTED IN IT?

NO → Farm it out. Hire someone or delegate it, or, if there is no other way, just do it and reward yourself with a high five.

YES, AND

DO YOU HAVE THE INFLUENCE?

NO → Then this is not your issue. Find a way to "own" it or let it go.

YES, THEN →

EMPLOY A PROBLEM SOLVING TOOL

"The man who moves a mountain begins by carrying away small stones."
~ Confucius

Consider the importance of the small stones of scaffolding and supporting students in the assessment process. How can you help students design their own assessments that provide them with opportunities to showcase their progress?

_____
_____
_____
_____
_____
_____
_____
_____
_____
_____
_____
_____
_____
_____
_____
_____
_____
_____

HOW TO HANDLE FEEDBACK

Feedback is a mixed blessing. It is necessary and valuable,
and can be hard to hear and hard to deliver.

Ask before you tell - "Would you like some feedback?"

 Studies found that phrasing it like this results in better acceptance and a change in action. "I'm giving you these comments because I have very high expectations and I know that you can reach them."

Start with what you see right and then what you want to learn.

 Say "This is what you do that helps me, this is what does not help me. What do I do that helps you and what does not help you?"

How can we do BETTER what we are already doing?

 Make it specific, and follow up with them. Use the 5 W's and an H - who, what, when, where, why and how-as inspiration.

FEEDBACK FORMATS

When giving or receiving feedback, it is helpful to do it in question format. Questions have solutions or answers, and that is what is needed when a change is required.

Some open ended question starters are:

Using these starters can prompt conversations that bring about real change.

What might be all the.....
How to....
How might we....
It would be great if....

Bonus points if you can ask multiple questions, looking at the same challenge from different ways.

Reflect on a current or past assessment. Using the open-ended question starters above, write 10 questions you might ask a student to start an engaging feedback conversation. It would be great if....

_____

_____

_____

_____

_____

_____

_____

_____

_____

_____

"Youth need coaches, not critics."

~ Amit Kalantri

Consider the importance of providing guidance, support, and encouragement to students rather than simply assessing and grading their assignments. How can you approach assessments and evaluations as a coach or mentor rather than the keeper of all the right answers? Think about a time when you've witnessed the impact of coaching versus criticism in the classroom. How did adopting a coaching mindset contribute to the growth, confidence, and motivation of your students?

_____

_____

_____

_____

_____

_____

_____

_____

_____

_____

_____

_____

_____

_____

_____

_____

_____

_____

When we are trying to evaluate ourselves or a situation, it can help to have a process. Here is a great example called PPCO. Let's give it a try! Think about a current idea: it could be a problem, a class project, or a house improvement design. Under each column, write down the pluses, potentials, concerns, and finally, ideas for overcoming those concerns.

PLUSES	POTENTIALS	CONCERNS	OVERCOMING CONCERNS
Write down all the things you like--all the parts that are good or on point.	Write down all the things that could happen because of this. Phrase them as "I might.." or "It might..." etc.	Write down all the potential problems and road blocks. Phrase them as questions by starting with "How to..." or "How might..."	Come up with many solutions for each concern, then choose the best one or the one that you are going to try first. Remember, you can go back and try another one.

Then you can write out your refined plan or idea. Try starting with "What I see myself doing is..."

_____

_____

_____

_____

_____

*"Our children need to know that we believe in their
ideas and potential as change agents."*

~ Germany Kent

Consider the importance of fostering a belief in students' abilities to assess their own ideas and potential as drivers of change. How can you cultivate an environment where students feel valued, supported, and empowered to assess and reflect on their own learning and growth?

_____

_____

_____

_____

_____

_____

_____

_____

_____

_____

_____

_____

_____

_____

_____

_____

_____

_____

WEEKLY CHECK IN

Choose at least three days this week you will spend doing something creative.

◯ ◯ ◯ ◯ ◯ ◯ ◯
s m t w t f s

This week I'm going to focus on ways I can encourage my curiosity and creativity in my classroom:

1. _____

2. _____

3. _____

Three things I am grateful for:

1. _____

2. _____

3. _____

WEEKLY AFFIRMATION:

CHALLENGE OF THE WEEK

How might I embrace curiosity and creativity to manage, monitor, and modify my personal learning?

_____

_____

_____

_____

_____

Personal goals for this week:

_____

_____

_____

_____

Professional goals for this week:

_____

_____

_____

_____

A DIFFERENT KIND OF CHECK LIST

Checklists can boost creativity by having us consider and reconsider.
Many people find joy in editing or refining the process.

Checklists can also be more than to-do items. They can also be thought/idea provokers.

Consider these, and add more.

○ How would my hero do it?

○ Who needs to know?

○ What would I think if I looked at this upside down?

○ How to make this cost effective?

○ Where else can I do this?

○ How would an alien handle it?

○ How much time have I allowed for it?

○ _____

○ _____

○ _____

○ _____

○ _____

**THINK ABOUT THESE WHEN YOU ARE
EVALUATING YOURSELF, AN IDEA, OR A SITUATION.**

SCAMPER

Are you familiar with the SCAMPER model?

This familiar evaluation tool can be useful both personally and professionally.

The SCAMPER model can be a powerful tool for bringing positive change and innovation to your professional and personal life. Here are some specific examples of how you can apply each element of the SCAMPER model:

S **SUBSTITUTE**: Identify areas in your routines or habits where you can substitute old methods with new ones. For example, you could substitute watching television before bed with reading a book to improve your sleep quality and overall well-being.

C **COMBINE:** Look for opportunities to combine different aspects of your life to create something new and exciting. You could combine your love for cooking with your desire to learn a new language by taking a cooking class in a foreign cuisine.

A **ADAPT**: Be open to adapting to new situations and challenges. If you usually follow a prescribed route home, try taking a new way home every day.

M **MODIFY:** Find ways to modify your environment or surroundings to boost your productivity and creativity. This could involve rearranging your workspace or adding plants and natural light to create a more inspiring atmosphere.

P **PUT TO ANOTHER USE:** Think about how you can repurpose items or skills in your life for a different use. For instance, you could repurpose old furniture into new DIY projects to unleash your creativity and give your space a fresh look.

E **ELIMINATE**: Consider what aspects of your life are no longer serving you and make a conscious effort to remove them. This could involve decluttering your physical space, cutting out negative influences, or letting go of limiting beliefs.

R **REVERSE:** Challenge yourself to look at situations from a different perspective by reversing your thinking. Try thinking of the world's worst solutions for a challenge, then doing the opposite.

By incorporating the SCAMPER model into your personal life, you can foster a more creative and adaptive mindset that will not only lead to positive changes but also open up new possibilities and opportunities for growth and innovation.

Eberle, R (1971) SCAMPER: Games for Imagination Development. Buffalo, NY: D.O.K. Publishers

Practice each of them here:

S

C

A

M

P

E

R

"Teaching kids to count is fine, but teaching kids what counts is best."
~ Bob Talbert

Reflect on your experiences with education and learning, particularly focusing on the values and the lessons that have significantly impacted your personal development. How were you assessed? What was really assed? What lessons do you remember the most and why?

Consider the difference between simply acquiring knowledge and understanding the deeper significance of what you've learned.

Bloom's Taxonomy has gone through revisions, and critics still argue its effectiveness. But, at its core, it reflects the importance of identifying achievable learning goals.

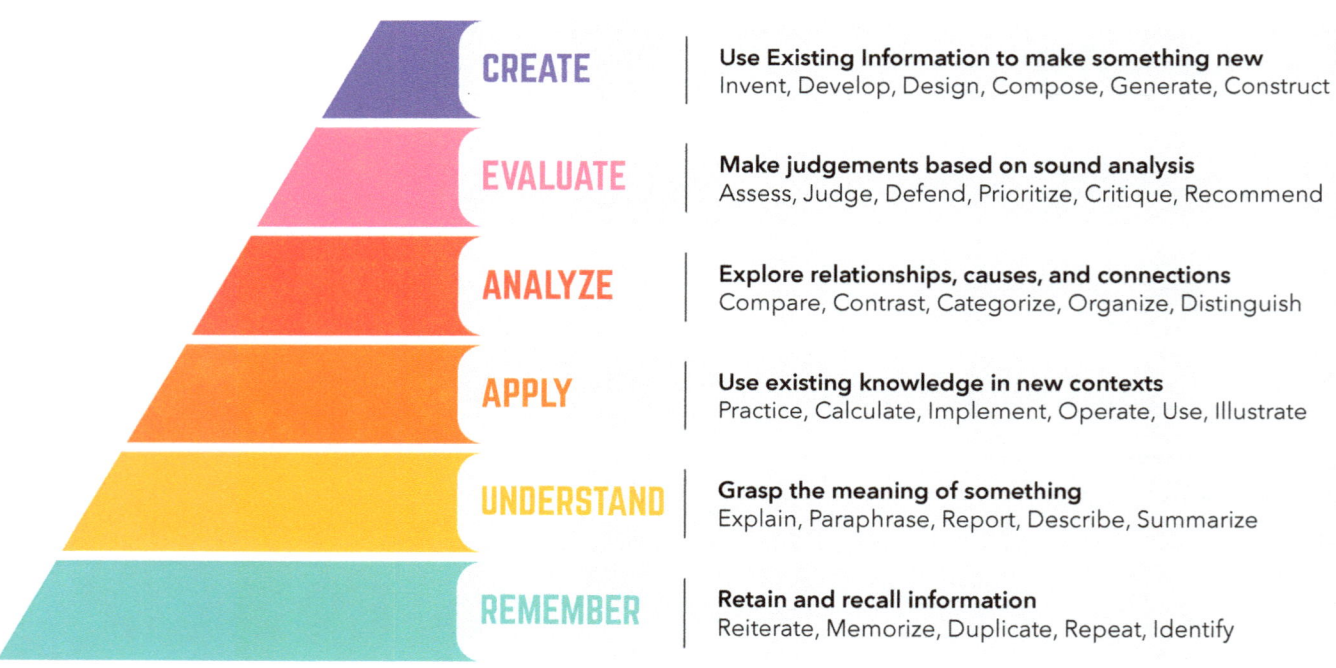

CREATE
Use Existing Information to make something new
Invent, Develop, Design, Compose, Generate, Construct

EVALUATE
Make judgements based on sound analysis
Assess, Judge, Defend, Prioritize, Critique, Recommend

ANALYZE
Explore relationships, causes, and connections
Compare, Contrast, Categorize, Organize, Distinguish

APPLY
Use existing knowledge in new contexts
Practice, Calculate, Implement, Operate, Use, Illustrate

UNDERSTAND
Grasp the meaning of something
Explain, Paraphrase, Report, Describe, Summarize

REMEMBER
Retain and recall information
Reiterate, Memorize, Duplicate, Repeat, Identify

Bloom, B. S. (1956) Taxonomy of Educational Objectives Handbook 1 New York: Longman.

Reflect on a past or current lesson, or a unit plan. Using Bloom's Taxonomy, does this progression of skills need to be revised? Consider if all assignments need to fall under create and which need the foundation of remembering in order to progress to the creation stage.

"An education is not so much about making a living as making a person."

~ Tara Westover

Think about the role of self-reflection and self-assessment in fostering your personal growth and development. How has that made you who you are today?
Consider the idea that education encompasses more than just acquiring skills for employment but also involves the development of one's character, values, and identity. How does helping students to self-assess their learning prepare them academically and personally for the world?

_____

_____

_____

_____

_____

_____

_____

_____

_____

_____

_____

_____

_____

_____

_____

_____

_____

Changing the way we do things can cause us to feel uncertain, nervous, and anxious. The way we assessed students in the past may not work anymore and that can be difficult at times. Sometimes, just writing down all the issues we think may arise will allow us to think through solutions. When you write about them below, make them open ended questions. This will help you process them in a proactive manner - and you will be able to see how to deal with these fears. Start each one with How to..., How might I..., What might be all the ways I.... to get yourself started.

UNCERTAINTIES

_____
_____
_____
_____
_____
_____
_____

ADVANTAGES TO NOT KNOWING

_____
_____
_____
_____
_____
_____

CONGRATULATIONS!

What shifts will you make in your teaching?

Now that you have come to the end, reflect on your biggest takeaways.

Which habits will you develop, personally and professionally, going forward?

"I WASN'T BORN TO 'JUST TEACH,' I WAS BORN TO INSPIRE OTHERS, TO CHANGE PEOPLE, AND TO NEVER GIVE UP; EVEN WHEN FACED WITH CHALLENGES THAT SEEM IMPOSSIBLE."
—UNKNOWN

Author Information

Katie Trowbridge

Katie Trowbridge is the President and CEO of Curiosity 2 Create. She has over two decades of experience as a teacher and mentor. Before becoming a teacher, Katie worked in marketing, public relations, and event planning. Throughout her career, Katie has focused on helping her clients and students find their best selves. In addition, Katie uses creativity to teach social-emotional learning, creative problem-solving, communication skills, team building, and personal well-being.

Her love for learning and research started at Luther North High School in the heart of Chicago and carried over as she earned a B.A. in English from Southern Illinois University. Years later, Katie wanted to focus on making a difference in the lives of teens and furthered her education by receiving a Master's in Teaching and a Master's in Education Administration. She is currently pursuing an Ed. D. in Innovative Teaching Strategies from Northeastern University.

Katie's passion for these areas allowed her to start non-profit organizations, assist school districts in writing SEL curricula, design programs for adults and students to encourage collaboration and communication, and mentor new teachers to find their voice. As a result, Katie has won several Teacher of Excellence and Outstanding Educator awards.

As a mom in a blended family, Katie works hard to bring an energetic, joyful, and creative spirit to her children and grandchildren. She finds time to embrace creativity through crocheting, painting, writing, and reading fiction.

Beth Slazak

Beth is the Senior Director of Education Programming at Curiosity 2 Create and has spent time at every level of the education world, from Elementary to college, instructing minds in the tools and techniques of creativity. She holds a Bachelor of Arts from the University of Buffalo in History, and in Dance, a Social Studies Certification in Education from Buffalo State University, a Master of Science in Creative Studies from Buffalo State University, an MBA from D'Youville University, and a three-year Certified Humor Professional Certification from the Association of Applied and Therapeutic Humor.

Beth has a passion for improv and has enjoyed studying and performing it at Buffalo ComedySportz and Toronto Second City. She is also a member of the Applied Improvisers Network, a group devoted to bringing improv off the stage into the world to help everyone work and learn better together, and has been able to work with groups in Italy, Mexico, Canada, and here in the US doing just that.

Beth has used her knowledge of deliberate creativity to help others recognize their value and tap into their knowledge and preferences, leaving the world a better place.
Beth has three children and two sons-in-law, and an amazing husband and a spoiled dog named Wednesday. She lives at a YMCA Camp because her husband is a camp ranger, and uses the summer staff as sounding boards for her program ideas.

CHELSEA STENVIG

Chelsea is the Junior High and Urban Specialist at Curiosity 2 Create and has a heart for serving others. Originally from the Chicago area, she earned her bachelor's in secondary education and English from Concordia University Wisconsin and a master's in Leadership and Innovation from Wisconsin Lutheran College.

Chelsea formerly taught English at New Berlin Eisenhower High School in New Berlin, Wisconsin as a long-term substitute but then quickly realized her heart was in the inner city. She taught all subjects in 5th grade at the Institute of Technology and Academics in Milwaukee, Wisconsin for one year and then became the 6th-8th grade ELA teacher and also spent time teaching writing and social studies. Chelsea later became the Dean of Students at ITA, where she coached teachers in classroom management, and lesson engagement and led a variety of professional developments for staff regarding student engagement and classroom management.

Chelsea was selected by the Center for Urban Teaching to participate in their leadership training program in which she learned to coach teachers and then became a co-principal during two summer school programs. She was selected to participate in the first cohort of a master's program through the Center for Urban Teaching and Wisconsin Lutheran College, in which she obtained a Master's in Leadership and Innovation, which focuses on turning around failing urban schools or starting up high-performing urban schools.

Chelsea moved to Knoxville in 2016. She loves spending time with her two school-age children, especially outdoors, hiking and camping.

CURIOSITY 2 CREATE

Curiosity 2 Create is a not-for-profit education organization created by teachers for teachers. We are dedicated to helping educators, schools, districts, and communities increase engagement by infusing deeper thinking and problem-solving into their classrooms.

We are here to help you:

• **Heighten student engagement** by captivating minds and encouraging deeper-level thinking

• **Empower your teachers** with empirically-based methodologies rooted in research

• **Retain your teachers** to rekindle their love for teaching

Want to join a community of like-minded educators united to amplify creative thinking and classroom engagement? **Join the Creative Thinking Network** (www.curiosity2create.org), a platform designed to empower teachers with the knowledge and tools necessary to integrate creative thinking into their classrooms while still maintaining academic standards. Imagine a classroom environment where students are not just passive learners but actively engaged participants, motivated to excel. The Creative Thinking Network aims to create such environments by equipping teachers with the skills they need to foster these qualities in their students.